'Ed Walker's attractively written
ment and determination can b
human needs. I have for many ye... ....pe
into Action homes. Long may this excellent charity grow and
flourish!'
Jonathan Aitken, former cabinet minister, ex-offender and prison
chaplain

'I've admired Hope into Action for some time, not least because it
has a holistic depth to it. This book both highlights the needs in the
UK and inspires us to realize we can actually do something. My
hope is this important writing will challenge and encourage people
and churches right across the country.'
Rt Revd Rowan Williams, Baron Williams of Oystermouth, former
Archbishop of Canterbury

'Ed has passionately pursued God to bring love, hope and freedom
to those in our society who are ignored, sidelined and forgotten. Ed
is honest and open, and his love of others shines through. However,
this is not a comfortable story; it shows that the grind of bringing
hope and love doesn't have quick-fix answers. *A House Built on Love*
will challenge you to generate hope into action for those in need. I
dare you to read it.'
Mandy Marshall, co-founder and Director, Restored Relationships

'Ed Walker's personal story is exciting and challenging in equal
measure. The charity he leads, Hope into Action, is creatively
pioneering a significant Christian response to the urgent housing
needs of the UK. I recommend this book wholeheartedly.'
Martin Charlesworth, CEO, Jubilee+

'A powerful and inspiring story of the gospel at work in today's world. There is so much here to encourage us all regarding the power of the Church and the potential for transformation in the lives of those most in need in our society.'
Paul Harcourt, National Leader, New Wine England

'I highly recommend *A House Built on Love*. Hope into Action links the local church with the homeless community and with some of the most broken. This book will build faith and encourage perseverance, and be a transforming tool to encourage more people to fulfil the good works which God has called them to do.'
Roy Crowne, Executive Director, Hope Together

Ed Walker graduated from Exeter University. He then worked for nine years with Tearfund in war and drought disaster zones, serving displaced and malnourished populations in a number of regions, including Burundi, Sierra Leone, Liberia, South Sudan, northern Kenya and Darfur. His final post was as Director of Tearfund's programme in Darfur, operating in one of the world's most dangerous environments.

After his time in Darfur he worked for three years in Peterborough, before giving up his position to start Hope into Action.

Ed is married to Rachel ('Rach'), a nurse. They have three children: Iona, Elana and Jos. They live in Peterborough and attend Bretton Baptist Church.

A HOUSE BUILT ON LOVE

The enterprising team creating
homes for the homeless

Ed Walker
with Elizabeth Batha

First published in Great Britain in 2020

Society for Promoting Christian Knowledge
36 Causton Street
London SW1P 4ST
www.spck.org.uk

Scripture acknowledgements can be found on page 252.

British Library Cataloguing-in-Publication Data
A catalogue record for this book is available from the British Library

ISBN 978-0-281-08119-6
eBook ISBN 978-0-281-08120-2

1 3 5 7 9 10 8 6 4 2

Typeset by Fakenham Prepress Solutions, Fakenham, Norfolk NR21 8NL
First printed in Great Britain by Jellyfish Print Solutions

eBook by Nord Compo

Produced on paper from sustainable forests

To those whom society has dishonoured, rejected, isolated and passed by

Jesus was and is homeless.

He was born in a borrowed stable: homeless.
He fled violence and lived as a refugee: homeless.
He had nowhere to lay his head: homeless.
He died rejected and betrayed, buried in a borrowed tomb:
homeless.

He identifies himself with the needs of those on earth today,
saying, 'Whatever you did for one of the least of these brothers
and sisters of mine, you did for me.'
(Matthew 25.40)

We, the Church, have billions of pounds' worth of 'loaves and fish'.
We have enough to provide every homeless man and woman with a home.
We also have something far more precious than that: love.
Just imagine what our God could do if we placed even a fraction of
these resources in his hands.

He would do more than you can imagine.

Contents

Contents

Contents

Foreword

In March 2017, at Ed Walker's invitation, I attended the Hope into Action annual conference. This was unlike any conference I had ever participated in before. I had first met Ed a few months earlier, when he told me something of his story and the background of the charity. I had been impressed, but nothing had prepared me for what I was to experience that day in Peterborough.

I came away overwhelmed by the power of the stories I heard. They were first-hand accounts of lives transformed. I had the privilege of handing out awards to some of the charity's tenants who had excelled during the last 12 months. Here were men and women who had experienced the transformational power of the gospel, not simply in a spiritual sense, but also in a deeply practical way: their lives had been completely restored and turned around for good.

This is Ed's story, and the charity's story, but also the story of numerous individuals whose lives have been touched by Hope into Action. Not all are 'success stories': there are moments of disappointment, pain and rejection; things haven't always gone well; mistakes have been made. The journey from opening one home for released prisoners in 2010 to having over 75 homes with 200 tenants and a turnover of over £1 million is not a smooth upward path, but it's a human adventure of faith and great hope.

As I listened to the stories told at the 2017 conference, I realized that the Hope into Action model, which so impressed me that day, was to establish *homes*; it was about treating people as individuals and responding to individual needs. And the results are extraordinary, with 90 per cent of ex-offenders not returning to jail.

But here is a story which also brings a challenge to the Christian charity sector, where some have lost confidence in sharing their faith for fear of losing government grants. Hope into Action is unashamedly Christian; the homes are open to those of all faiths and none, but a local church or cluster of churches is central to the well-being of each house. In these homes, people discover that they are loved and treated as precious in the midst of their mess, rather than being made to wait until they have sorted themselves out.

This book is also a challenge to each of us in our approach to finances. Ed is passionately encouraging us to consider how we could seek to unlock the wealth many of us have stored up in bank accounts, ISAs, pensions or property. Could it be better invested for the advancement of the kingdom of God?

Ed's book is inspiring, encouraging and at times a little uncomfortable to read, but it is saturated with deep wisdom and insight regarding the human condition and how we, as individuals and churches, can meet people where they are rather than where we would like them to be.

Steve Clifford
Former General Director, Evangelical Alliance

Foreword

This book will challenge readers in the very core of their being. Ed Walker takes us on his journey from Darfur, where he had served with Tearfund, to his emerging new work among homeless people in the UK. With him, we are slowly confronted with the totality of God's call on our lives; we too hear God speak into our faith, values, relationships, attitudes, money, lifestyle, purpose and future.

Yet Ed expresses all this not in preaching mode, but by gently sharing stories of encouragement, insight and hope. He is as ready to confront his own experience of being deskilled and disempowered ('writing with his weaker hand') as he is to share the amazing fruit of God's blessing on people without resources, security or hope. The result is a wonderfully heartening and powerful book, told by a gifted storyteller. Time and again, Ed finds exactly the words and metaphors needed to convey the characters, context and plot of his narratives and bring situations alive.

But more than Ed's ability to take us into people's lives, it is the vision of God's calling and equipping of a Christian believer which grips the reader. The experience of God's compassion and provision fuels Ed's energy and enables him to move on in faith. It helps him to identify the reality of poverty, seeing it not simply as practical and material, but also as relational – a state in which people have nowhere to go and no one to go to. It helps him to identify the limits of what God asks of him: not to change lives but to help provide the environment where people can find the hope and motivation to bring about change. Starting a charity from scratch to provide homes for the homeless, including ex-prisoners, is no simple undertaking. But Ed's book shows what can be achieved when it is approached through unconditional, non-judgmental listening, and brought under trust and faith in God's love.

Do read this and pray. Buy copies for your whole church. And see where God might be leading you.

Elaine Storkey
Writer and broadcaster

Telling a story

Hope into Action was set up to provide love and homes for those who find themselves homeless. Our desire is to empower those individuals and to help in the process of restoring their God-given identity.

For some, telling their story, or having their story told, leaves them feeling exposed. For others it can be empowering, even cathartic, to hear, read or tell their story. Knowing how to judge what is best in each case is not always easy.

My desire to tell someone else's story must always be overridden by that person's right to choose what is made known about his or her experiences. The needs and wishes of the individual involved supersede ours. For this reason, there are many amazing stories of people's lives that will never be told; there are some disclosures that will be carried to the grave as secrets. It is absolutely right that this is the case. Their stories are theirs alone.

On the flip side, many of our tenants do want to share their stories. They want to explain, they want people to understand and they want to help.

There are a few individuals in the Gospels whose names we are never told. I used to think it a pity that people hadn't bothered to name the 'adulterous woman' or the 'bleeding woman' and so we know them only by their 'sins' or 'shames'.[1] Now I wonder whether the writers deliberately protected them or their families by keeping their names a secret.

Following the same line of thought, I have, in places, altered names, circumstances, locations and timings in order to protect the individuals whose experiences are covered in this book.

Stories bring issues to life and, as my editor has continually reminded me, make for interesting reading. There are many parts of my story I would rather not have told, as this book is not meant to be about me but about the people I have met, the churches that share God's love, and the Jesus I have learned so much about on my journey. I hope that in all of it, I may be transparent and Jesus will shine through.

Acknowledgements

The story of Hope into Action is the outcome of the prayers, work, investment, support, wisdom and donations of a great number of people. I am just one of hundreds committed to the vision of the organization.

It is hard to single out any individuals, as by doing so I fail to mention others. However, Noel Garner, Keith Nicholson, Sarah Vassiliades and Kate Doran-Smith have all been on staff for at least six years at the time of writing, and are towers of personality, strength, drive and passion. All are co-leaders with me on the Executive of Hope into Action. Gavin Howard, Yvonne Emery and Gavin Bateman were trustees at the beginning, and continue to be sources of support and encouragement. Their friendship, input and wisdom have been amazing. Jenny Rayner, an empowerment worker extraordinaire, has been with us since the very first days and accompanied me in many of the early 'stories' in this book. Thank you, all.

I am also grateful to those who birthed this book. Editor Tony Collins saw potential in a sea of structural confusion and grammatical errors.

Tony also found Elizabeth Batha to help write the book with me. The original drafts were very different from the current book. What started as a mosaic of unchronological thoughts and writings has been crafted into a sequential story. Although I wanted to keep myself out of the text as much as possible, Tony and Elizabeth convinced me otherwise.

Elizabeth is a master of her trade, drawing out of me what was really going on, adding attention to detail and applying mastery of the English language, combined with determination, flexibility and good humour. She has always been a joy to work with.

Acknowledgements

Lastly, among all those involved, the most honour must go to the heroes and heroines in this book (and the hundreds of other tenants we have housed who are not mentioned). Few can understand the courage and tenacity they have shown. My admiration for their strength of character is immense, and I am profoundly grateful to them for letting their voices be heard. Through them, I have met and found the living Christ time and again.

Introduction

Many, LORD my God, are the wonders you have done, the
things you planned for us. None can compare with you; were
I to speak and tell of your deeds, they would be too many to
declare.

–Psalm 40.5

Why have I written this book? The answer, in part, is to draw attention to the many amazing things that God has done. On numerous
occasions along the journey of Hope into Action, I have experienced a sense of marvel as I have seen the hand of God at work.
I find my heart resonating with the words of the psalmist: 'Make
known among the nations what he has done. Sing to him, sing
praise to him; tell of all his wonderful acts.'[1]

Over the last nine years I have often felt my jaw drop, and I want
to share these moments in the hope that they will encourage and
inspire others. When I hear a former addict say, with beams radi-
ating from his face, 'Jesus is better than any drug,' I sense heaven
has kissed earth; something stirs inside me, and I feel inspired to
declare what God has done. I want to share the wonder that occurs
when heavenly power and love encounter someone low in esteem
and high in shame in such a spectacular way that it becomes the
apex in his or her life story: the fulcrum on which one side of that
person's life was a 'before' and the rest an 'after'.

Words cannot adequately express the wonder of such a moment.
Yet they are the medium we are blessed with as we seek to convey
our sense of amazement at who God is and what he does. As Jesus
said, if the disciples did not speak out their praises for him, even
the rocks would cry out. Words are the means we possess to try to

describe the awe we experience, deep in our core, as we meet God and see his hand at work. They are the way we seek to express how we feel as we reread part of the gospel and understand afresh, with yet deeper amazement, how radically loving Jesus is.

Naturally, our hearts are drawn to dwell on the joy we experience as we stand on the mountaintop, marvelling at all we survey around us. Yet with mountains come valleys. Likewise, our journey has had its fair share of moments marked by discouragement, stress and despondency. I don't want to gloss over these. They are part of the rollercoaster ride that has carried us to where we are today. The Bible heroes – Joseph, Moses, Daniel, Esther and countless others – knew great challenges alongside great victories.

While I hope this book will inspire many – echoing the words of John: 'so that it may be seen plainly that what [we have] done has been done through God'[2] – it is intended to be more than just a record. I hope it will further the conviction that the Church has something distinctive, something special and something necessary to offer the vulnerable and homeless in the UK. Quite apart from the obvious spiritual benefits that the Church brings, it offers something sociologically unique. I hope that reading this book will give you confidence in the vital role that churches can, and I would say should, be playing in the homeless sector.

I use the phrase 'homeless sector' as it is often used by professionals. However, homeless people are not a sector. Nor do they particularly need more professionals. They are people: individuals made up of DNA, genes, synapses, emotions, hearts, brains and feelings. In other words, they are human beings. Therefore, they need love. They need to feel they have a home, and they need to belong; they need to believe they hold innate value, and they need someone to believe in them. Put another way, they are almost exactly like you and me.

For all its faults and foibles, nothing competes with the Church in bringing people of diversity together week after week after week.

More go to church on Sunday than attend football matches on a Saturday. Nowhere else do you find men and women, rich and poor, black and white, old and young, and even ex-con artists and ex-cops, joining together – albeit imperfectly – over one cause. When the apostle Paul penned those radical words that there is neither Jew nor Gentile, slave nor free, male nor female, for all are one in Christ,[3] perhaps he pictured something like our present-day Church. Certainly, he lit a radical philosophical fuse that, for two millennia, has inspired the belief that we can all be one. Since the homeless are included in that 'one', and since they are in need of love, the Church has something special to offer. It can offer a people who care about (not just for) those in need, who ask after them, who take them for coffee, who counsel them and who laugh with them. Likewise, the homeless have much to give the Church, and the Church becomes richer and more complete when the homeless are included in that 'one'.

Think of the home where you grew up. If you are lucky, you found there love, nourishment, boundaries, guidance, grace, forgiveness and much more. The homeless are not called 'houseless', even if it is often the case that they are not sleeping in a house. What we all need is a home: all facets of a home.

I hope you will be encouraged by what God has done and what the Church can do. I also hope you will be encouraged to know that we are blessed in our own walk with God as we step out to respond to those in need. I passionately believe that we grow in our understanding of God as we encounter Jesus in the poor.

Not that it is always easy to put ourselves in the way of such blessing. The other day, I met a woman who has been a Christian all her life and has lovingly supported no end of good overseas causes. However, she was honest enough to express her reluctance to be involved in Hope into Action's work. As she delved deeper to unravel her reticence, she was able to recognize that the root of her hesitation was a fear of the people we work with. The unknown is often accompanied by an immobilizing hurdle of anxiety. A core message of this book – and indeed the life and teachings of Christ – is that we meet God when we meet strangers.

From his birth to his death, Jesus presented a message of inclusivity. He met, prioritized and touched those from 'the other side':[4] the foreigner who came as a wise man, the 'lowly' shepherd, the sceptical snob Nathanael, the divorcee, the ostracized and homeless man possessed by a legion of demons, the man suffering with leprosy, the 'unclean' woman, the prostitute, the adulterer, the tax collector, the Canaanite woman, the Zealot, the prodigal, the Samaritan, the disabled. He continued right up to his death, touching both a criminal being crucified by his side and a foreign centurion standing below him.

As we follow Jesus' example, sharing bread with those we previously feared – those 'on the other side' who are strange to us – we find that we ourselves grow. We experience love rising from within, driving out fear. We grow in our fullness as human beings. We discover that our sense of humanity increases as we meet and eat with Christ himself. Jesus taught us this in a most extraordinary way in the parable of the sheep and the goats.[5] He identifies himself with the stranger, the sick, the naked, the hungry, the thirsty and the imprisoned, and then hits us with the startling line: 'Truly I tell you, whatever you did for one of the least of these brothers and sisters of mine, you did for me.'[6] Such a personal identification with humanity stood in stark contrast to how the Greek gods were portrayed in the culture of that time, as we see in the stories of Zeus and Hercules. As the writer to the Hebrews reminds us, when we stretch ourselves to show hospitality, we may encounter angels themselves.[7]

The journey of Hope into Action has many parallels to Jesus' famous miracle of the 'feeding of the 5,000':[8] we saw a need, doubted we could do anything about it, took our small offerings, placed them in the hands of Jesus and watched him multiply them.

Again and again we have seen resources, in the form of houses and other assets, being directed by him, and we have rejoiced to see people filled with life-giving food. Not to say it all happens without some work on our part. If we are following in the footsteps of the disciples, we can expect to be pouring ourselves out. I often ponder on how exhausting it must have been for them to wait on 5,000 people.

I have not written this book to provide a comfortable read. In contrast, my hope is that it will act as a stimulus to reassess our involvement in society and to open our eyes to see as Jesus sees. Look a bit harder on your way to work. Stop and observe as you go to the shops. Homelessness is in the shadows. Walking by on the other side of the road cannot be an option. If we are all made in the image of God, then we are all equal. One person's suffering is one tragedy too many.

If we need inspiration, we could do worse than meditate on the six words Jesus wove into the Lord's Prayer: 'Give *us* today *our* daily bread.'[9] We were not taught to pray for 'me' or 'my' daily bread. 'Us' and 'our' refer to the entire current and future human race. This leads to a table-turning solidarity with our fellow humans. Let us strive to share our gifts and wealth so that all people, be they male or female, rich or poor, gay or straight, black or white, may find themselves in a just, safe and loving environment in which they can grow and learn.

1

New horizons

Take the first step in faith. You don't have to see the whole staircase, just take the first step.

–Martin Luther King Jr

Masterei, Darfur, Sudan, February 2008

The cool morning air was rapidly fading away. Soon the temperature would climb to blistering levels, cloaking us in suffocating heat.

I sat on a large outcrop of rock, gazing down at the market in Masterei. I watched the hustle and bustle as the beleaguered population took advantage of the few hours of truce afforded by market day. Here I could see people from all strata of society, distinguishable by the height of the animals they rode. My eyes fell on a group of women, their swathes of clothes a riot of colour, selling a few last provisions to a group of men loading their donkeys. The donkey owners were the privileged ones. Most never reached such ranks, getting by with nothing more elevated than their shoes – or even just their bare feet. As I looked down, I could see the elite, with thin scarves wrapped over their faces to shield them from the sandstorms, riding in on stallions and camels. I watched as they dismounted, took down their guns, slung them over their shoulders and walked into the market. It was like the Wild West on speed, Sudan style.

I had scrambled up the ten-foot-high rock earlier in the day, when the temperature had been more conducive to such efforts. By my side was my colleague Tim, who was soon to take over the reins from me in leading and supporting the Tearfund teams in Darfur.

Now we were perched in a perfect spot to survey our surroundings. I gazed out across the land that had been the backdrop to the challenges and rewards of my efforts to bring some humanity to the ravaged lives of the people of Darfur.

We had time on our hands. It was our day off, and there was nothing to do in Masterei but wait for the heat to abate, after which we'd be able to take a walk as the African sun set over the sandy Chadian plains to the west. It was the ideal moment to review our past and look ahead to our futures. Tim knew what lay before him. It was here, in front of his eyes. My future lay off in the distance, hazy and unknown.

My mind reflected on the scenes that had made up my life here in Sudan for the last three and a half years. I thought back to my meeting the day before with the leaders of one of the many armed rebel groups: all wearing bandanas, bullets strapped to their chests and AK-47s dangling over their shoulders; all looking about 14 years old.

I thought about how such negotiations had become so much more complex over my time here. When I first arrived, most of the area had been controlled by the 'Government of Sudan' militias known as the Janjaweed – 'devils on horseback' – a name arising from their attacks that killed hundreds of thousands and forced millions from their homes. Their control of the area had at least given a relative sense of calm and security at that time. Now they had splintered, as had the rebels, and there was a cross-border war with Chad, a land just visible in the distance. As I scanned the scene around me, I estimated that within six miles of our location there were at least six separate armed groups, factions or rebel forces.

Within that same area was the scene of the most disturbing security incident I had experienced in all my nine years of working in war- or conflict-affected areas. In my early days here, we had been able to carry out our humanitarian activities with the expectation of respect. But that had all changed on 1 September 2005 when our

Tearfund convoy had been attacked and our staff members person-ally assaulted: beaten with rifle butts, threatened with guns to their heads and subjected to sexual violence.

I looked down to my right. Less than 500 yards away, I could see the compound of the United Nations (UN) peacekeeping force, with its tall barbed-wire fence, large block of concrete across the driveway – to prevent drive-in suicide bomb attacks – and high wall behind. The security measures weren't without reason: a few months earlier a rebel group had launched a rocket-propelled grenade through the compound and killed a UN peacekeeping soldier.

I shifted my gaze to my left, where I could see our own compound, with its bamboo fence and no protection other than a gate. We previously had two large four-wheel-drive vehicles stationed there, but now we just used donkey carts to get around the town. We had changed our policy after another rebel group (not the ones we had met yesterday or the ones who had attacked the UN) had stormed our compound, forced our staff members on to their knees and held guns to them until the keys had been handed over. As far as we knew, both vehicles were now being used in the cross-border war with Chad.

Tim and I reflected on how crazy this scene was, how hard it would be to explain it back home and how privileged we were to have lived through these past years. This was my final trip to Darfur. In total, I had lived and worked in Sudan for six years. Its climate and topography were the hardest of any I had known, and the incidents and 'evil' (for that is what it was) I'd experienced, either directly or vicariously, had left me emotionally marked. I still loved my job and life, and was upset at the thought of leaving. Yet my wife, Rach, and I somehow knew it was time to go. Our prompting had come as we had read the book *If You Want to Walk on Water, You've Got to Get Out of the Boat*.[1] We had both felt convicted that our current environment had become our 'boat'.

3

I loved and respected Tim as a man, a friend and a colleague. It was a joy to be handing over to him, and I knew he would do a better job than I. The sun was now rising and I breathed in, savouring, as if for the last time, the sights and sounds below me. Then we slunk off the large rock and started sauntering back. We both avoided talking about work, which had dominated so much of our conversation over the past couple of years.

As we got near the compound, Tim said to me, 'You'll never have anything like this in the UK, Ed.'

'I know,' I replied sadly.

It was true; I loved my life here. The future in the mists of the horizon is harder to love than the present in one's clear grasp. Uncertainty, apprehension and doubt tugged at my confidence as I looked ahead. But when you sense the call, you have to try to follow. No matter the joys and challenges, striving to be in the centre of God's will is the inspiration and aspiration of all who want to follow Jesus.

It was time to step out of the boat. A new adventure awaited.

2

The man on the bench

When Jesus landed and saw a large crowd, he had compassion on them.

–Matthew 14.14

We arrived back in the UK while Rach was pregnant with our second child. After reconnecting with our native land through a caravan trip, which included taking our daughter Iona to Iona, we settled in Peterborough. As with any move, we missed parts of our old life and took time to adapt to our new. Perhaps one of the hardest elements was losing the sense of meaning and purpose that comes from working overseas. We had been invested in the country where we lived, working for an organization we believed in, on a programme we both loved, running projects that added enormous value.

However, some things were a definite improvement: playgrounds, for example. When we lived in Khartoum (the capital of Sudan), I hadn't found a single park with kids' equipment for Iona to play on. So, to pass time, I would walk her down dusty streets, trying to excite her by pointing out the odd stray bird or maybe . . . Well, I can't think of anything else I would distract her with. Most children her age back home could mimic the 'voices' of farmyard animals; she would simply make a donkey sound every time we heard the bells of a milk cart hustling down the other side of our high compound walls. Arriving in Peterborough, she spent endless hours climbing rope ladders, growing confident on slides, whooshing on swings and engaging in no end of other adventures.

While my little girl was enjoying this part of our transition, I was wrestling with other aspects of it – in particular, how our lives fitted into our new and very different surroundings.

During the six years I had spent in Sudan, the Scripture verses that inspired, sustained and strengthened me the most were from Isaiah 58:

Is not this the kind of fasting I have chosen:
to loose the chains of injustice
    and untie the cords of the yoke,
to set the oppressed free
    and break every yoke?
Is it not to share your food with the hungry
    and to provide the poor wanderer with shelter –
when you see the naked, to clothe them,
    and not to turn away from your own flesh and blood?[1]

A few verses on, the passage continues:

The LORD will guide you always;
    he will satisfy your needs in a sun-scorched land
    and will strengthen your frame.[2]

I can vividly remember trying to work out how those key verses related to the UK in the twenty-first century. 'How, God, do these words apply?' I would pray. In coordination meetings in Khartoum, we would regularly discuss our response to the destruction of villages and the resulting displacement of thousands of people. My first coordination meeting with the council in Peterborough involved listening to a woman passionately arguing the need for improved playground provision in the city.

Really?

'Is this what I have to get enthusiastic about now, God? How exactly do my favourite verses become relevant here? I know you must need Christians in this city, but to do what, exactly? What should a Christian be doing in a place such as this?'

The verses seemed to apply so aptly to Sudan, where one's passion would so often run hot and one's sun-scorched frame would need strengthening. Windy fenland Peterborough, by contrast, felt cold and somewhat muddy.

All such existential wrangling subsided in autumn 2008 when Rach heroically produced our second beautiful daughter, Elana. I set about recovering from the particularly long and traumatic labour, while Rach manfully nursed and fed our new bundle of joy and vulnerability, who somehow, already, held such power over our hearts.

One morning while on paternity leave from my new job, where I was working with hostels for the homeless and young people's projects, I was merrily playing with our first daughter in yet another playground we'd found, this time near the city centre. The autumnal air was still fresh, yet to be fully warmed by the rising sun. Suddenly I noticed a man sitting on a bench by the edge of the play area. He looked a bit like a tramp (if you will excuse the term) but not quite; he was clean, his beard was short and his hair looked recently washed. We got chatting and I asked him his story. His experience was typical of what thousands of people go through every year in the UK. He had left prison that morning, full of hope and determination for a fresh start. As he was leaving through the external gates, the prison officer said to him, 'We'll see you back in three months' time, mate.' At which point, his fragile self-esteem crumbled as he faced the reality that he had nowhere to go. He had taken the £47 prisoners receive on discharge and, by the time I met him, was halfway through a bottle of something pretty strong. He had probably made a logical decision. What else was he to do? What would I have done in his shoes?

'Where were you before you went inside?' I asked him.

'I was in Cambridge.'

'Why don't you go back to Cambridge?'

He rolled his eyes at my naivety. 'Because if I go back to Cambridge, I'll end up surrounded by the same old mates in the same old hostel and I'll end up back inside in three months' time.'

'Well, don't worry,' I said. 'I'll try to help. I work with three hostels.'

My naivety persisted. I presumed I would be able to sort this. His eyes, however, betrayed a better understanding of the system. I couldn't trace a glimmer of excitement in them.

I phoned each hostel right there and then. None would accept him: 'He's too old.' 'We don't take ex-offenders.' Dispirited, I tried one in Norwich: the same response.

As I finished my last call, the man stared back at me with cold indifference. It wasn't despair; it wasn't acceptance either, just a reluctant resignation to his life situation.

I could do nothing for him. I strapped Iona back into the child seat on my bike and cycled off. I left him there.

As I departed, I was struck by two emotions: first, disempowerment, a very different feeling from the one I had been used to overseas, and second, anger. In my mind's eye I could see over a dozen churches within a mile's radius of this playground, situated as it was next to Her Majesty's Prison (HMP) Peterborough. All those churches are filled with people singing songs every Sunday and reading the Bible each week. The songs and the Bible are full of verses about a God who loves the ostracized. Where was the connection? Why were none of the churches reaching out to the rejected here on their doorstep? Where was the outworking of all that love for God if none of the churches were doing anything about giving the homeless a home?

I had read several times in recent months that giving ex-offenders a home reduces their reoffending rate by 80 per cent. The need was there. Why, then, was no one doing anything about it?

Then I remembered those verses from Isaiah: 'Is not this the kind of fasting I have chosen: to . . . break every yoke . . . and to provide the poor wanderer with shelter?'[3]

I had just met a 'poor wanderer'. Was God answering my frustrated and confused prayer?

Upset as I felt at the time, I never imagined how this encounter would set me on a track that would so seriously change my life: how it would lead me into the path of danger and draw me to the extremes of society as I engaged with both the overlooked and the rich and famous. I also had no idea how it would dent my finances, affect my family and steal my sleep. Yet neither did I imagine the way it would lead to peaks of joy, spiritual insights and God-ordained provision.

3

An early taste of prison

The poor make the party.

–The Bishop of Burnley

While I was still overseas, thinking and dreaming (and maybe praying a bit) about what to do when we settled in Peterborough, I had felt some stirrings of interest in becoming involved somehow with prisons – in a ministry rather than an internment role. I was therefore pleased to discover, first, that our new home was less than a mile from HMP Peterborough, and second, that a prison chaplain was coming to speak at the church we had started attending, Bretton Baptist Church.

The chaplain, Andy Lanning, was short and stocky with a neatly trimmed beard. He spoke with passion and grit. He told us of a man he had ministered to in prison who had come to faith and become a regular member of the worshipping community that met there. This man had left the prison a changed person. A few weeks after his release, he was found dead in a shed, having suffered the effects of hypothermia and an overdose. No one had been there for him on release.

Could this really be the case? I questioned. In 2008, people are dying for lack of shelter? Isn't this the space the Church is called to? As Christians, we know people have been leaving prison since the time of Joseph and Pharaoh – have we not cracked this one yet?

I went to chat to Andy after the service. It wasn't long before he was giving me a tour of the prison. I volunteered to join his Bible study with the prisoners on a Wednesday evening. I loved his passion, his humour and his desire to see the kingdom come.

He would tell us numerous stories of those he was working with – and often refer, angrily, to how the churches needed to do more to support ex-offenders. His anger was contagious.

I walked in on my first week conscious that, in the eyes of the prisoners, I looked like an 18-year-old with arms about half the size of theirs. My image issues were compounded by the complete lack of tattoos on my body. I wasn't too sure whether they would accept this posh, young, weak-looking bloke.

For the most part I just sat and listened, but Andy was good at asking me questions and drawing me in. On that first Wednesday he got me to say a sentence or two about Darfur. I didn't quite know what angle to come in at, but I mentioned some of the violence, thinking it might help me win over these hardened men. All the prisoners tutted or shook their heads, showing disgust. I couldn't quite work out whether their indignation was genuine or feigned. Had they not committed similar crimes?

Some weeks later I started chatting to one of the prisoners and felt such a strong connection during the conversation with him that I was deeply moved. We then sang a worship song standing side by side, both of us belting it out. It was a powerful, Holy Spirit moment.

After the guard had led all the prisoners back to their ward and cells, I was left clearing up with Andy.

'So, erm, Andy,' I began, 'that guy I was talking to and standing next to in worship?'

'Yeah, I know the one.'

'Erm . . . he seems a really great guy. What's he in for?'

Andy looked sheepish. He shuffled his weight from one foot to the other and kept his eyes on the floor as he carried on cleaning up.

'Erm . . . well, he would be in for sex offending.'

It turned out the whole bloomin' room was in for sex offences. Andy had grown that worshipping community of sex offenders to well over 30 men.

I left prison that day feeling highly conflicted. I actually felt physically sick in my stomach. That night I went for a prayer walk with Elana. She was still only a few weeks old, so I wrapped her up warm in a sling and paced round the local park, trying to reconcile the bond of fellowship I had experienced with this man and the disgust I felt at his crime. After a while I remembered the parable Jesus had told about a rich man throwing a party.[1] No one came, so he sent messengers into the streets with orders to invite the blind, the lame and the beggars.

It is God's party, I reasoned, so he can invite anyone he wants. We're all invited; some say no, and so he goes to those who say yes. (I later told that story to the boys at the exclusive Harrow School and said the invitation to the best party was there for them as well; sex offenders had heeded the invite – why not them?)

In fact, it is more than just an invitation. Jesus told the Pharisees, 'When you give a banquet, invite the poor, the crippled, the lame, the blind, and you will be blessed.'[2] As the Bishop of Burnley argues,[3] it is 'the poor who actually make the party'; without them the banquet would not have been blessed. The poor still make, or should make, the feast of God complete.

I've often wondered why Andy didn't brief me on the prisoners' crimes beforehand. I suspect that would have been prison protocol. I'm grateful he didn't. By not doing so, I was able just to see and meet my fellow man. Our joint humanity connected us, and I was undistracted by their crimes or, to put it more accurately, my reaction to their crimes. This experience taught me an important principle that we still use today in Hope into Action: don't look at the file before you go in. Meet the person first.

4

An unconventional memorial

Say not in grief that she is no more, but say in thankfulness that she was.

–Rabindranath Tagore

At the same time as visiting the prison, I was getting to grips with my new job working with young people and local hostels. One balmy Sunday evening as I was walking to work, I saw a bunch of guys who lived at one of the hostels sitting outside the local pub, and I stopped to join them. Holding court was Peter Sullins, a rather unconventional man with a beard, who seemed capable of handling both his drink and a decent conversation at the same time. I enjoyed his company and the way he could engage in argument with thoughtful and articulate reasoning. He was well known in the hostel. Many of the residents were fond of him, though others found him threatening. Among the staff, he was known for his difficult behaviour and his tendency to butt heads with the management.

About six months later, James, a close friend of Peter, went to visit him in his room. He found him dead. Shock waves ricocheted through the hostel.

Although Peter was well known in his community, he had no relatives, and it was decided he would be given a public health funeral at a crematorium outside town. Sadly, I was away that day and unable to make it to the service. I returned to hear a very dismal account of the occasion. Only three people had turned up, and the ceremony had been completely non-religious and had lasted all of 15 minutes. How dreadful, how drab, I thought. Was that what he deserved? Was that what anyone deserved?

I compared this pitiful farewell with what I had seen in Africa. Even in the refugee camps there had been guidelines on how care should be taken over burial rituals. I had witnessed first-hand the importance of honouring those who had died and the dignity that this bestowed. I had seen how vital the cultural and religious expressions of burial and remembrance were in enabling the community to grieve.

By contrast, Peter's public health funeral seemed so empty. It somehow expressed a sense of spiritual void. The pervasive British paradigms of 'we don't do God' and 'we don't talk about God in case we take advantage of the vulnerable' left in their wake a vacuous emptiness.

I felt Peter deserved more than a public health funeral and that we could honour him more appropriately by holding a memorial at the hostel. I decided to ask my minister, David Whitlock, if he could hold the service, and called him up to put the proposition to him.

'Ed, I'm really busy right now . . . Do I have to?'

I understood how he felt and left it there.

The next day my phone rang. It was David. He would do it.

On the day of the memorial, there was David, standing in the hostel lounge with a ragged collection of about 30 people. There were more piercings and tattoos (not to mention cleavage) on display than you would normally see in church on a Sunday, and I wondered if David had ever led a service with such sights on offer.

David led us beautifully, drawing a parallel between King David, the soldier revealed in the Psalms, and Peter, who had also served in the armed forces. David hadn't just prepared a message; he had taken time to meet Peter's friends and find out about him. He pitched the tone, verses and feel absolutely right. Then he paused and asked the men and women gathered there if they would like to share any memories.

A bold move.

How would we respond?

The six seconds of silence felt like a lifetime – or even two lifetimes. I watched in admiration as David held the silence, but I could sense he was beginning to panic.

Then suddenly a woman began: 'Peter was a great friend of mine...'

I expected the rest of us to listen and nod our heads solemnly and pensively as we digested her words. Instead, everyone in the room began sharing his or her thoughts with the nearest person. No one seemed to be paying any attention to anyone else, yet everyone was talking as though someone was listening. It was like 30 people shouting down their individual mobiles. No one seemed to understand that it was protocol to stop talking after a couple of pithy, winsome sentences. From silence, we had ascended into holy remembrance cacophony. David was still panicking, though now for a different reason. Would he ever be able to call order? Eventually, he regained control and quickly brought the memorial to a close.

I headed to the buffet laid out on the pool table, loaded up on sandwiches, and then wandered over to the corner of the room to a man who was standing alone. I guessed he was about 5 feet 8 inches tall and around 17 stone (240 lb), with at least 16 earrings in his left ear alone. I was feeling a bit awkward and, as I took a bite of sandwich, plumped for my middle-class conversation card number 3: 'So how did you know Peter, then?'

He paused and thought. Then he turned to me and said, matter-of-factly, 'He used to have sex with me.'

Out flew the sandwich.

I looked at the man's plain poker face. To this day, I have no idea whether his reply was brilliant deadpan humour or the truth. I still also have no idea what I should have said next. Fearing my social skills were inadequate for the next exchange, I made my excuses and moved on.

James, Peter's friend who had found him after he died, was also at the memorial. I had no idea at the time what an important part of my life he would become.

5

They were like sheep without a shepherd

Sheep without a shepherd go astray.

–Lailah Gifty Akita

I often start my talks with the story of the man on the bench, and people think I woke up the next morning and started a charity within a week. The reality was very different. That encounter stirred something within me and set off a train of thoughts. I started wondering: if a person reaches out with compassion and grace to all who fit the description of 'poor wanderer'[1] (my preferred description of someone in a homeless situation), what does that look like in practice? What are the needs of such people? Is that even the right question, or should we rather be asking: what are their strengths? Should we not view them as untapped potential – dormant 'assets' (a rather cold term, I agree) – for our society? How, then, should we respond?

I began reading academic papers that explored these questions. The researchers' answers could be boiled down to three things that the homeless need: somewhere to live, someone to love and be loved by, and something to do. It's as simple and complex as that.

As I applied all this thinking to the man on the bench, I came to see that the physical expression of his poverty – his homelessness – was only a symptom. The cause of his physical poverty was relational poverty. In other words, he had nowhere to go because he had no one to go to. In contrast, if I left prison tomorrow, I could go to my friends, relatives and wife (if she'd still have me – she says she would). This man had no one to go to and, because of that, was probably experiencing a depth of loneliness most people reading this book cannot relate to. If we were to do a causal analysis of people who find themselves homeless, we would find at the root – sometimes buried very deep – a relational poverty and deficit of love in their lives. No one is, or can survive as, an island. To quote God's first recorded observation about our primary needs: 'It is not good that man should be alone.'[2]

I kept analysing the man's situation and trying to work out what a good response should be. A worker from a charity specializing in alcohol misuse, I reasoned, would say he needed help with his drinking; someone from probation services would say he needed help with his behaviour; a food agency volunteer would offer him some food; a debt advisor would offer counsel about his debts; someone from a housing organization would assess him for a bed; an outreach team might offer him a blanket; an evangelist might come along and say he needed Jesus. A bloke called Isaiah, though, might encourage us to break *every* yoke in his life, and address all of the above needs. He might call us to look beyond the obvious poverty and see the causes behind it. Thus, we might need to consider not only the immediate physical needs, but also all the cords of oppression that had caused and sustained them. Our job, then, would be to walk hand in hand with this individual to break every yoke and see him attain his full humanity and flourish into his full potential.

Could I, with the right resources, have changed that man's life? I came to realize that I could not change anyone's life – apart from my own, and even that only painfully slowly. I could, however, try to provide an environment where he was likely to find the necessary hope, motivation and determination to make his own choices for positive change. I could, perhaps, try to provide a safe, secure home and positive, loving relationships and then walk with him through the ups and downs of his journey. I came to hope that at the heart of who we all are – of who this mysterious man on the bench was – is innate strength and, somewhere, a will to fight, strive and thrive. What might happen, then, if someone trusted him with a home and believed in him? Thriving might look different for each individual. For him, it might mean being able to get a job and pay his bills by standing order; or perhaps, for that phase of his life, washing, doing the weeding and putting on some new socks would have been progress. I began to sense that when love breaks into a heart, it creates a transformational energy that brings hope, and that this hope then brings to birth self-motivated action.

I looked at how Jesus used the words from Isaiah to articulate his own ministry, announcing that he was anointed to proclaim good news to the poor, freedom for the prisoners and recovery of sight for the blind, and to set the oppressed free.[3] If that is how Jesus described himself and the needs he was responding to, surely it must also be relevant to the Church's mission statement.

I concluded that it would be important to reflect the same good news to those who are oppressed and poor. I started imagining being able to say, 'Come along to our home. Let us try to work with you on those issues that oppress you. We believe if you engage in positive relationships, you might find yourself doing okay.'

I also saw, as I looked at the hostel system, a focus on beds rather than homes. I noticed that the high rents taken from residents to cover the overheads of large organizations made it difficult for them to find employment; this, in turn, could lead to people being stuck in hostels, where it was hard to engage in positive, enriching relationships.

I realized that people coming out of prison obviously weren't the only ones these Scripture verses applied to. I came to see many other needs. My reading led me to hundreds of thousands of people who are poor wanderers in the UK: over 4,000 sleeping on the streets; over 40,000 asylum seekers; over 10,000 who have been trafficked; over 100,000 coming out of rehabilitation centres or combating addiction; over 70,000 sex 'workers', many with class A drug addictions; thousands more suffering domestic violence – with about 150 people being turned away from refuges every week.

My thoughts continued to develop: if Christ is to operate through us as his body here on earth, so that we see such people as Christ sees them, and we share his compassion for them, what should that look like? How do we, as the Church, rise to the challenge of shepherding them, feeding them and healing them?

6

A more subtle compassion

I am alone, surrounded by unbelieving activists and inactive believers.

–*Shane Claiborne,* The Irresistible Revolution, *2007*

My experience of moving back to the UK felt strangely reminiscent of the times I had moved overseas. Each time I changed country, I had the feeling I was writing with my weaker hand. Things took longer; I didn't know where the shops were; the one-way system seemed odd; I got lost. Then at work there would be a new culture, a new language, a set of issues whose history I didn't know and a raft of TLAs (three-letter abbreviations) to learn. Feeling like a foreigner in your own land is a strange experience. I thought hard about things others took for granted, I asked a lot of stupid questions and, occasionally, I spotted oddities with unusual clarity of vision. Some of my initial perspectives could be quite insightful, but most reflected my poor understanding. The problem was I never knew which thoughts to have confidence in.

So it was that when I moved back to the UK in 2008, I noticed a number of things about the Church and its position in society. It took me a while to articulate what I was recognizing, and still longer to have confidence in my assessment. However, I was repeatedly aware that the Church was under attack. Every time I heard something pertaining to Christianity on the radio, followers of Jesus were being forced to defend themselves: someone was criticizing them; they were on the back foot. It struck me that while every football team needs to have a sound defence, it only actually wins by attacking and scoring goals.

I saw that the UK Government was providing a great deal of money to the charitable sector, but that the tone attached to much of it was that there should be no religious input. There was an implicit, and often explicit, assumption that speaking to the vulnerable about spiritual matters somehow automatically amounted to abuse. I reflected it had been easier talking about my faith while working in Khartoum under conditions of sharia law than it was in Peterborough.

I was also struck by a form of secular–spiritual divide. On the one hand, I saw many charities that had been established by Christians but no longer spoke about faith, battered down as they had been by government and by cultural and legal regulations. Then, on the other hand, I saw churches that had once operated in the social action space but had retreated (for lack of confidence or expertise) and were now choosing to concentrate more on 'proclamation and evangelistic activities'. (I am glad to say that the situation has changed significantly since these initial observations, with the enormous rise in ministries such as food banks and street pastors.)

I saw this divide even in my own immediate world. I was working full time for a charity helping young people, and in my spare time I also helped with a youth Alpha Course at my church. In that capacity I took our young people from church to a week-long Christian youth event called Soul Survivor, where we heard amazing testimonies of young people's lives being touched and changed by the Holy Spirit. When I got home and returned to my job, I heard great stories of the work we were doing there as well. Yet there was no intersection between the two areas. Why is no one mixing the two? I wondered. Imagine what might happen if we combined the spiritual with the professional!

After about a year of living in Peterborough, I found these thoughts were becoming increasingly intrusive. I began to question my core beliefs. Could a person really do effective, holistic, intelligent outreach and also talk about Jesus? Were all spiritual conversations with the 'vulnerable' automatically abuse? Did such people not also have the right to hear the good news of Jesus?

As these thoughts and feelings grew in intensity, I decided I needed to take time off to pray and think. I made my way to Peterborough Cathedral, stunning in its grand dimensions – 145 feet high and 480 feet long – and beautiful with its intricate carvings and breathtaking stained-glass windows. Its grandeur and splendour were almost too overwhelming, so I sneaked into a side chapel to find a quiet spot. Wanting to re-examine the Gospels and see how Jesus did it, I took out my Bible and turned to Mark: I reckoned it was the shortest Gospel so I could get through it the quickest. Then I took out a piece of paper, drew two columns, and wrote the headings 'miracle and didn't talk about faith' and 'miracle and did talk about faith'. Then I read through Mark and noted down the accounts that fell into the two categories. As I reached the end of the Gospel, I reviewed my list: 16 miracles, in 13 of which Jesus talked about faith or the kingdom of God.

I continued staring as I thought about the implications. I am a follower of Jesus, I reasoned. I base my outreach on his. If he shared about faith as he ministered, I should do the same. I rose slowly and began walking, still thinking. As I exited through the west-facing arches into a setting sun, I resolved that I would follow Jesus and his way of doing things. If I couldn't find a charity that married spiritual understanding with good outreach in the city, I was going to have to start one.

Thus, I was aware of another, more subtle need: not just the need on the streets, not just the need for churches to do something, but also the need for a form of outreach that was genuinely holistic. I took my inspiration from that moment in the synagogue in Nazareth when Jesus declared that he had come to release the oppressed *and* proclaim the good news.[1] Surely, I reasoned, if we are seeking to represent him on earth, we should also be representing both these aspects of his mission.

There were many, many times over the coming months and years when I either doubted my conclusions from that visit to the cathedral or was scared by their implications. However, for the rest of the day I was on a spiritual high, and my mind began excitedly exploring the path I wanted to take. Both overseas and in the UK, I had encountered a lot of Christian outreach, and I started drawing on my experiences to develop an approach that I felt would be appropriate. I didn't want to operate with a sense of arrogance, I reasoned. I had felt discomfort at times over the sense of superiority I had seen displayed in both the evangelical 'right' on the one side and the liberal activists on the other. I had found that the approach of both these sides could feel hollow or incomplete. Was it possible, I wondered, to start something that would reflect the beliefs I had come to value: a humility to learn from everyone, while challenging norms and systems; a heart to listen to the homeless, while also proclaiming Jesus is Lord; a depth of spirituality that is attractive, loving and true, while burning with an inner passion that fires one's heart and drives one's love? Could I create something that never lost those Christ-like central tenets of 'releasing the oppressed' and 'sharing the good news' – something that expressed them in an appropriate, sensitive way, while holding in the heart a sense of mutuality? That was the challenge I was beginning to feel called to. It excited and frightened me.

7

It began with a prayer

Come with me by yourselves to a quiet place and get some rest.
–Jesus in Mark 6.31

It took a long time for my thoughts, experiences and ideas to percolate through and to crystallize. I would now say it was a process of God working in me. The Christian language for it might be that I was developing 'a sense of calling'.

While it is true I was wrestling with all the things I have described, if you had analysed my prayer life it would have revealed much more about my desire for promotion, extra money and extra responsibility than it would any genuine desire for the poor, the Church or, frankly, following the Lord's will.

The fulcrum, the point at which Hope into Action was birthed, was the night I decided to submit my flawed and fallen will to God's. I was at Soul Survivor, with its large celebration evenings at which the Holy Spirit often moved in amazing ways. In my case, though, God didn't speak to me in one of the main events. Rather, it was when I was left on my own to babysit while everyone else in our group was out enjoying the party atmosphere. I normally love camping, but that evening, lying on my bed in the dark, dank night, surrounded by a thousand other tents and aware that everyone was having more fun than I was, I felt distinctly grumpy.

For some reason, I had brought along a book called *Issues Facing Christians in Sudan Today*, a tome of over 400 pages. As I was wading through it, one particular, very simple sentence struck me between the eyes: 'Prayer is submitting your will to God's, not the other way round.'[1]

In that moment I realized my entire prayer life was about me trying to get God to endorse my will for my life. I was actually treating him like my servant, when obviously the complete opposite should be the case. As I combined this revelation with my swirling thoughts about the needs I had seen and my conviction that the churches should be more fully engaged, I sensed I had to do something in response.

I reconnected with the incredible words of Mary: 'May it happen to me as you have said.'[2] I also reflected on the wonderful promise from the Psalms: 'Take delight in the LORD, and he will give you the desires of your heart.'[3]

As a response, I formulated a prayer that I resolved to pray every day for the next six months: 'Lord, put on my heart your will for my life, and give me the courage to follow.'

It was a prayer that I found terrifying – because I already had a hunch about where it might lead.

8
Doubt steps

> Hope has two beautiful daughters; their names are Anger and
> Courage. Anger at the way things are, and Courage to see that
> they do not remain as they are.
>
> *–Augustine of Hippo*

I think my expectation was that by the end of the six months I
would have the following:

1 a totally clear business plan that had fallen out of the sky
  (perhaps through a vivid dream that led me to a crystal-clear,
  bona fide, definitely-from-God 'no doubts' vision);
2 a massively rich donor who would fund the work and my salary,
  plus quite a lot of extras, on a five-year, upfront basis.

However, neither of these came to pass. I can see now that if they
had, it would not have benefited my faith. (Though I do remember
penning a letter to Bono asking if he would consider item 2!)

So what did happen?

I marked six months in my calendar and noticed it was a few
days after my sister's wedding.

I not only prayed; I also chose to fast for one day a week. Not
major fasting by any means: mostly just missing breakfast and
lunch before stuffing myself in the evening, but fasting nevertheless.

I went to conferences on related topics and prayed for guidance.
Once, I accidentally planned a fast for a day when I was at a conference. I quickly learned, given the copious amounts of free food, to
avoid doing that again.

I read the Bible more, and with a deeper hunger, as I searched for God's voice. I learned verses and memorized inspiring quotes, including a favourite one from President Theodore Roosevelt:

It is not the critic who counts; not the man who points out how the strong man stumbles, or where the doer of deeds could have done them better. The credit belongs to the man who is actually in the arena, whose face is marred by dust and sweat and blood; who strives valiantly; who errs, who comes short again and again, because there is no effort without error and shortcoming; but who does actually strive to do the deeds; who knows great enthusiasms, the great devotions; who spends himself in a worthy cause; who at the best knows in the end the triumph of high achievement, and who at the worst, if he fails, at least fails while daring greatly, so that his place shall never be with those cold and timid souls who neither know victory nor defeat.[1]

Nothing much happened for the first few months. But then I slowly found I could not stop thinking about the idea of starting a charity. My every spare thought seemed to be given to mulling the issue over and over in my mind. I would wake up thinking about it; I would fall asleep wrestling with it. I told no one but Rach.

Around Christmastime I was three to four months into my six-month commitment to prayer. Bono had still not replied. Neither had the billionaires I had found on the internet who had also received beautifully crafted letters. So what was I to do? Should I assume this meant a great big 'No' from God? That would certainly be more convenient. I could then stop all this childish daydreaming, make a few more mature and pragmatic career choices, and crack on.

The only problem was that the thoughts were not going away. By now they felt more like a monkey on my back, and not just any old monkey – quite a heavy one. Maybe even an orangutan. I felt as though my shoulders must be an inch or two lower than normal, and my head seemed bowed with the weight of these ideas. Was this just a symptom of not being happy elsewhere, or were my thoughts something I genuinely needed to respond to?

I came to see it was unlikely that gold would drop from the sky in the next two or three months, and that perhaps, instead, God wanted me to do some stepping out. So I planned the first of my terrifying steps of doubt: I wrote to my minister, David (who had led the memorial in the hostel), to see if he had any time for me to share my crazy ideas. He said he liked crazy ideas, and before long I was sitting in his front lounge wondering what on earth I was doing there. I imagine he was too.

After the obligatory British small talk, I began. He must have listened to me for about 20–30 minutes without saying a word. I poured out some convoluted waffle and ended my ramble with the plea: 'Please tell me this is *not* from God and then I can continue with a normal career.'

I'll never forget David's gentle response: 'I can't tell you it's not from God.'

Drat!

'Go away and speak to two or three other people and see what they say.' In other words, test the seed in some soil. At this point Hope into Action was barely a tiny seed.

I followed David's advice and approached some carefully selected potential allies, each time in trepidation.

My first target was Yvonne Emery, an entrepreneur and property coach with as fast a mind as you will encounter.

Her response: 'Why haven't you started this thing yet?'

Gulp. More fear.

I then chatted to my friend Andy Lanning, the prison chaplain, who I knew was passionate about issues of this kind. He suggested we meet at 5 p.m. for a beer. He ordered his usual, a Stella – the namesake of his 4-foot 11-inch wife – and then walked away chortling to himself as he joked, 'Small but mighty.' We sat down, and he eventually stopped chuckling. I began. I was into my second sentence when he interrupted, 'Uh oh – this sounds like a God thing.'

Yikes. Now I was really getting scared.

My third approach was to Gavin Bateman, an ex-RAF commander with a no-nonsense character, a big brain and very astute spiritual discernment. More encouragement.

My final contact was Gavin Howard, a man with a massive passion for social justice and a beautiful heart. He didn't tell me I was mad either!

After all these conversations, I went back to David and told him what had happened. We discussed it further, and then I blurted out a cunning plan. 'David,' I confidently exclaimed, 'I think what we need to do is call a meeting with lots of local churches and form a committee.'

'Ed,' came the winsome response, 'the last thing you should do is form a committee.'

'*What?* Why not?'

'Instead, gather two or three passionate people around you and go for it.'

That was a piece of advice I will never forget. If the seed had found some soil in meeting Yvonne, Andy and the two Gavins, David was clearing that soil of weeds and gently dropping in some rain of wisdom and encouragement. God, David reasoned, didn't send a committee; he sent a man, Jesus of Nazareth. God, in fact, never ever called a committee. He always seemed to call one person. As I rummaged through my biblical knowledge, remembering Moses, Joshua, Esther and others, I realized that David perhaps had a point. Yikes. I was feeling scared again.

Even with all the amazing things that have happened since, I would still say that one of the biggest steps of faith I ever took was the next thing I did.

9

'I have no cows!' – a lie ricocheting down the ages

Jesus told them to make all the people sit down in groups on the green grass. So they sat down in groups of hundreds and fifties. Taking the five loaves and the two fish and looking up to heaven, he gave thanks and broke the loaves. Then he gave them to his disciples to distribute to the people. He also divided the two fish among them all. They all ate and were satisfied, and the disciples picked up twelve basketfuls of broken pieces of bread and fish. The number of the men who had eaten was five thousand.

–Mark 6.39–44

While I was praying and taking these initial hesitant steps, my mind was also busy ruminating on the issue of finances. An obscure trail of thought brought me to a fundamental conclusion, and it all started with the way the Dinka people of South Sudan talk about their wealth.

In my time with the Dinkas, I had learned that their wealth is measured in cows. For a Dinka man, the more cows you have, the more wives you can buy. Western feminists, I know what you're thinking . . . But it gets worse: the more wives you have, the more daughters you have, and the more daughters you have, the more cows you can buy when you sell them. Beauty in that culture is measured by height and darkness of skin. (I therefore felt secure when Rach, short and blonde, was working there.) The more beautiful the daughter, the more cows she earns you. Not only that, but the more wives you have, the more sons you have, and the more sons you have, the more people you have to look after your cows.

In 2000 I found myself in a vehicle with a commander from the Sudan People's Liberation Army (a rebel militia commonly known as the SPLA). I knew him reasonably well and was aware that he'd just bought himself a sixth wife. By all accounts, she was tall and dark. All this meant one thing: he must have had a lot of cows. With a long way still to go on our journey through the dry savannah, a lull in the conversation, and no other topics springing to mind, I offered him my congratulations on his recent conjugal arrangements. He received my comments with thanks and seemed warmed by them, so, feeling a wee bit cheeky, I carried on our little chat by remarking that six wives must mean he owned a few cows.

Quick as a flash he turned to me and, with a mischievous twinkle in his eye, replied, 'Oh, Ed, I have no cows.'

We both knew it wasn't true – but it was his way of saying 'I'm not going to tell'. He lied.

Over nine years later, the ingredient of this conversation, when mixed with wisdom from the Bible and seasoned with my own experience, helped me understand an innate human attribute concerning our money: we lie.

But we'll come back to that.

My time of prayer and fasting and my growing sense that God was calling me to start a charity happened just before the Conservative Party came to power in the UK; we didn't then know the charitable sector was about to face major funding cuts. We had been through the financial crisis of 2008, but government 'austerity' was just a word in a political campaign, not yet a hard-biting reality.

I was at a charity function at this time and found myself in a roundtable discussion on the subject of funding. I was struck, in particular, by a comment that came from a vicar who was also a trustee of a Christian charity. 'We realize', he asserted, 'that we shouldn't talk about faith in our charity, because doing so would harm our chances of receiving government funding.'

I thought about that comment a lot over the following weeks. Eventually, I came to see that it might be the right thing for that charity at that time. However, the main thing I kept returning to was the phrase 'holistic outreach'. To my mind, 'holistic' means seeing not just people's immediate poverty, but also those things, decisions and systems that oppress them and prevent them from fulfilling their true potential. It also, crucially, means recognizing that each individual has spiritual needs, and being open to meeting these in an appropriate and sensitive manner, alongside our other work. Many churches I encountered were not really dealing with the root cause of poverty. Rather, they were engaging in 'sticking plaster' outreach (which is still of benefit and often done with great love), followed, perhaps, by a sermon or talk about Jesus. On the other side of outreach, there were a number of charities that had been started by Christians but had almost completely lost any connection to the passionate proclamation that their founders began with, choosing instead to bow to the idol of government money.

Thus, up and down the UK, people have come to the conclusion that 'we shouldn't talk about faith because doing so would harm our chances of receiving government funding'.

In contrast, we read in the New Testament that a guy called Peter was faced with the same dilemma, only with flogging and incarceration thrown into the equation. When commanded by the local government to stop talking about Jesus, he promptly raised his voice in prayer, carried on some excellent holistic outreach in the middle of the thronging central market square, and boldly continued talking about Jesus, informing the authorities that he could not 'help speaking about what [he had] seen and heard'.[1]

Considering the role model of the vicar versus that of an ordinary but gutsy first-century fisherman, I knew which one I wanted to imitate. (By the way, I am not, at all, advocating that we throw away all diplomatic relations with the local council – quite the opposite. However, at Hope into Action we stand by a set of principles that we won't ever change or compromise on.)

Somehow, those words from that vicar crystallized my views about working with the marginalized in the UK. Despite all my English reserve, mixed with a deep instinct to conform, I too find myself unable to stop talking about Jesus. This reminds me of how Jesus said of his disciples, 'If they keep quiet, the stones will cry out.'[2]

I had supported outreach all my life, including excellent, intelligent work in dealing with the causes of poverty and empowering individuals to enrich their lives. However, I felt that such work should also be accompanied by a sharing of the good news of Jesus. I found precious little of that in the UK, and much of the reason was the fear of losing government funding.

I went back to the Bible.

While I was at Tearfund I had often spoken in churches, quoting the words of Jesus in Luke 4:

The Spirit of the Lord is on me,
    because he has anointed me
    to proclaim good news to the poor.
He has sent me to proclaim freedom for the prisoners
    and recovery of sight for the blind,
to set the oppressed free,
    to proclaim the year of the Lord's favour.[3]

In my talks I had highlighted the justice agenda within the verses, but now, as I read them again, I saw that the word 'proclaim' occurred three times within the short passage.

If I could hear one speech of Jesus, it would be the one contained in these verses. Jesus spoke as one who had been a refugee and was living under occupied rule. I can just imagine the electric passion, crackling conviction and Holy Spirit power that resonated through his voice, leaving those listening with neck hairs standing, terrifyingly, on edge.

Somehow Jesus encapsulates in 50 words what holistic outreach is. I cannot tell you how many times I have come back to those verses from Luke, stared at them, looked at them from a different angle, thought about how they apply to this country, and then tried to ingrain them into the approach of Hope into Action.

I boiled all this down to a simplistic 'faith statement' that I repeated to myself like a mantra: 'I believe in a God who is bigger than the Government. If you honour God by emulating a form of outreach that he modelled, then he will honour you with the finances for it.'

Every child in Sunday school would be happy with that simple truth. However, some things become harder to trust as you grow older.

With all these little steps, I edged my way towards accepting that I had a sense I was being called to start a charity, and that I would trust that God was able to grow and finance it.

After a while I began to ask myself the question: how? I thought through the realities of the situation: I am just one bloke; I don't have any resources to fund myself; I need to put food on the table; I am researching funders and there aren't that many out there; Bono still hasn't replied; I don't have a wonderful communications department to launch a highly successful national campaign; competition among charities is incredibly steep; Christians already give to a lot of needy causes. In real terms, how exactly might God do this? Where would this money actually come from?

Then one night, as I was lying in my bed, I had an epiphany moment. Thoughts began racing through my head and I couldn't sleep. It was all sparked by just one question: what is the value of the combined assets owned by Christians in Peterborough?

I began adding up the amount of Christian wealth that must be lying dormant in churches in my city. If that sort of money exists in Peterborough, I thought excitedly, then how much must there be in the country? What would happen if we could tap into and 'undam' this wealth? I found myself doing some maths: if there are 30 churches in this city, and each has 10 people who own a house, and each house is worth £100,000, then that is $30 \times 10 \times 100,000$, which makes £30,000,000 in assets. This was calculating on a conservative scale. In fact, there were more than 30 churches in Peterborough, I guessed there was more than an average of 10 people per church who owned a house (especially as one church had over 1,000 people in it), and the average price of a house in Peterborough was far higher than £100,000. So I knew £30,000,000 was nowhere near the total.

In the weeks that followed, I began looking up the amount that churches across Peterborough kept in their reserve accounts. While some churches had virtually nothing, plenty had tens of thousands of pounds in their reserves. I found one, relatively small, church that had over £250,000 in its bank account. Again I did the maths: 30 churches with an average of £30,000 in reserves would generate another £900,000.

What about the amount of money spent on worship equipment? If there were 30 churches, and each had managed to find £20,000 for its musical instruments and sound systems, then that would mean that churches in Peterborough had spent well over £500,000 on resources of this kind. Add on to this the worship expenditure of a megachurch and then the odd cathedral organ repair, and soon the total is not far shy of £1,000,000. These are assets that depreciate over time. Therefore, all we need to do, I reasoned, is focus on the Bible verses that say the kind of worship God desires is to loosen the chains of injustice, to share our food with the hungry and to provide the poor wanderer with shelter.[4] If church leaders cared as much about the poor as they did about acoustics, then we should be in.

I found my mind going down these alleys of thought and felt uneasy about it doing so. Was this blasphemous? Was it wrong to think in these terms? Wasn't worship central to what the Church does? I did not want to detract from the importance of expressing love, praise, adoration and more for God through song.

I'm not sure of the answers to these questions, but I do know that as I was mulling them over, I inadvertently fell upon these words from the Bible: 'Away with the noise of your songs! I will not listen to the music of your harps. But let justice roll on like a river, righteousness like a never-failing stream!'[5]

On and on my mind went, picking up these clues dropped from heaven, each pointing to unassuming rocks along the trail – but under each new rock was hidden a spiritual box of latent treasure. I saw a huge seam of money hitherto virtually unmined for the kingdom of God.

But where would I start? Where would it all begin?

The next clue oriented me to my own bank account. Rach and I were beneficiaries of an inheritance of £30,000. We had done nothing to deserve that money and we knew we were very lucky. For a few months we had been praying, 'Lord, how can we use this for your glory?' Prior to the financial crash in 2008, we had made a reasonable return on it. However, now it had gained only £30 in interest over one year. As we thought about the parable of the talents, we felt we were not really maximizing the 'talent' God had given us.[6]

We had told no one about this money. We had kept it absolutely secret.

Around this time, I was reading through the book of Proverbs and came across this verse: 'One person pretends to be rich, yet has nothing; another pretends to be poor, yet has great wealth.'[7]

I began joining some dots.

- **Dot 1.** Some bloke in a completely different culture was not going to reveal how many cows he had.

- *Dot 2.* I had a very strong instinct not to talk about my wealth.
- *Dot 3.* I find the same human characteristic observed and recorded over 3,000 years ago.

This is triangulation. This must mean that if Rach and I, who have only ever worked for charities or the UK's National Health Service (NHS), have money and are not talking about it, there must be others out there with wealth secretly stashed away.

It was this understanding of human nature, coupled with faith in a God who can multiply my five loaves and two small fish,[8] that was foundational to my confidence to start Hope into Action. I suppose anyone working as a financial advisor knows what I now know: that people conceal their wealth. However, back then I was not privy to such knowledge. I just had faith in God and in this revelation of the human instinct to conceal private money and possessions. My Dinka friend's claim, 'I have no cows,' was evidence of a lying habit that transcends cultures and ricochets down the ages.

10

Stepping stones of encouragement in a sea of fear

When Jesus looked up and saw a great crowd coming towards him, he said to Philip, 'Where shall we buy bread for these people to eat?' He asked this only to test him, for he already had in mind what he was going to do.

Philip answered him, 'It would take more than half a year's wages to buy enough bread for each one to have a bite!'

Another of his disciples, Andrew, Simon Peter's brother, spoke up, 'Here is a boy with five small barley loaves and two small fish, but how far will they go among so many?'

–John 6.5–9

It was now spring: the trees were in blossom, the air was warming and the days were lengthening. The Bangladesh national cricket team was about to tour England with Graeme Swann's spinning in its prime. I had just had the joy of seeing my daughters, Iona (three and a half years) and Elana (18 months), as (particularly cute) bridesmaids at my sister's wedding, and the happy inner currents from the glorious family event were still circulating strongly.

It was three days after the wedding and six months after I had committed to my half-year of prayer. I was at the other end of the step of faith I had taken after talking to David. It might not seem such a big step now, but trust me, at the time it most definitely felt that way. What was it I had found so difficult? I had called a meeting. Not everyone I had invited was able to be there, but with me were Yvonne, Andy and Gavin Bateman.

The meeting was a pivotal moment and, as such, helped me to articulate some of my ideas in a clear, concise way. As I sought to explain my thinking, I took a piece of A3 paper and drew a picture of a house with a homeless person inside it, linked both to an outline of a church that provided friends and to a professional worker (whom we now call an 'empowerment worker') who would ensure quality of performance. That picture, while not particularly artistic, remains true for Hope into Action to this day. The combination of church volunteers, wealth to buy a house, and a professional to ensure excellence remains our 'model'. It is a model that, while simple, has won awards from numerous professional bodies, including the NHS, a left-wing newspaper and right-wing think tanks. But more on that later.

By the end of the meeting, we had two agreed actions to move forward with:

1 to buy a house;
2 to start a charity.

I had little idea about the former and none about the latter. However, after discussion must come action. If the chat doesn't leave the realms of discussion, then it is no more than pub banter. Actions create energy, energy creates hope, and hope leads to more actions – which in turn create more energy, hope and action.

I would wake every day with a dozen good reasons not to implement those actions – investing a large chunk of money and our future security in a house for an ex-offender not the least among them. I would go into work every day praying this prayer: 'Lord, I'm really panicking today. I'm probably making a terrible mistake, but I'm going to carry on with these actions anyway. Please drop me some signs of encouragement.'

And that is what he did: he dropped some tiny stones of encouragement. I would step from one fragile stone to another. Never was my balance sure. At times, these stepping stones would lead me to dead ends. However, while I was following them, they served as encouragement, and by the time I realized they were dead ends, some other stones had appeared that I could step on to instead.

It was as though I was on some spiritual treasure hunt. Every day, I would watch desperately for God to drop me a sign. I would find a clue, pick it up, look at it, muse over it, and try to work out whether it was from God and what on earth it meant. In everything, I would strain to hear his voice, to understand what I should do and where I should step next.

During this time, I was greatly encouraged by the words given to another flawed follower, the ancestor of our faith: 'Go to the land that I will show you.'[1] As in my case, God did not give Abraham the GPS coordinates of his end destination as he set off. The message was: 'Just go and put your faith in me . . . and I will show you.' Likewise, I was heartened by the account of the feeding of the 5,000. I was reassured by the doubts, including money doubts, expressed by the disciples. I was encouraged to see that they were able to take those doubts to Jesus, and that Jesus still worked through them in spite of their failings.

Then I found myself in our church one morning when Phil Timson, a good friend and Baptist evangelist, was speaking. He is an excitable charismatic, and that morning he was feeling both excited and charismatic. He then did to me what I hoped he wouldn't do – he called me to the front, where people were being prayed for privately. Another excitable charismatic, Lizzy Standbrook, then began prophesying quietly over me, saying I would walk into a new field and open up a new way. She gave me a verse from Isaiah: 'Whether you turn to the right or to the left, your ears will hear a voice behind you, saying, "This is the way; walk in it."'[2] Lizzy's brother, Rich (a calmer version of his sister), then brought a prophecy for me – again speaking softly into my ear – about a new candle being carried into a new room.

Neither of these people had any idea about what I was doing or the context into which each of them was speaking. Neither knew what the other had said. Their messages served as another couple of clues, a celestial encouragement that got me through a few more days and kept some doubts at bay.

Every day, I was still trying to pray the prayer: 'Lord, put on my heart your will for my life, and give me the courage to follow.' It was a prayer inspired by King David's words in Psalm 37.4: 'Take delight in the LORD, and he will give you the desires of your heart.' Throughout this time I would often return to that psalm. It moves on poetically from verse 4 until the seventh verse, where it states '. . . wait patiently for him'. Those four simple words stuck in my head. Time feels longer when you are anxious or fretting, and I was doing both at this stage. For days my mind kept returning to the words 'wait patiently'.

As I was in this phase, my minister, David, came up to me and gave me a verse. (Hang on, I thought, don't give me a verse! That only happens to proper Christians with more importance and charismatic giftings than I have.) It was Hebrews 6.15: 'And so after waiting patiently, Abraham received what was promised.' Marshalling all my spiritual insight, I concluded that maybe God was telling me to 'wait patiently'.

These verses didn't mean I stopped working or stopped pushing forward with the charity. What they did do, however, was to comfort me. God was offering me a heavenly clue, a calming hand on my lead as I strained forward – reassuring me that maybe I wasn't going bonkers down here on earth. 'Keep pushing forward; things will come together!' was the message I was hanging on to.

I had been struggling to work out how to start a charity. I knew the Charity Commission had something to do with it, but that was about all I knew. I had phoned up friends who were lawyers, but they were not experts in charity law. I was still without a clue, scrambling around in the dark, when Gavin Howard happened to mention to me over a lunch that the way to start a charity was to go through an organization called Stewardship. That was the tip. The next day I was on the phone to these people, drinking in their expert advice and discovering the steps I needed to take.

I now started venturing further out with my ideas, meeting church leaders and sharing the vision of what we wanted to do. These were small stepping stones, but each bore my weight as I gingerly moved forward. They were not far apart; not once did I take a giant stride. I just got up each day and cautiously placed one foot in front of the other.

Thus began Hope into Action. Through it all, I knew that it would eventually require me to leave the security of my current job; that was always my biggest fear and worry.

Here was a moment in my life, and that's all it was – a brief moment, when I actually had to put my faith in God. Did I really believe he could provide? Did I really believe he could look after my finances? Was my faith really in him? During worship times, I would often think of the trust game where a person is blindfolded and has to fall back into the arms of a friend standing behind. This was the nearest I had ever got to falling into the financial arms of God. In reality, I probably only fell to about 45 degrees – nothing like the trust shown by many giants of the faith who have gone before or those now suffering for their faith around the world. Nevertheless, in those moments of reflective worship, I was able to reach the point of feeling safe as I was falling and of knowing I was going to be caught. (This doesn't mean I would get out of bed the next morning with the same feeling; indeed I would often wake up in the early hours with sweat on my back. However, I could turn my mind back to my experience during worship and find the courage for my next tiny, fearful step.)

The honest truth is – even if I hadn't realized it, or wasn't able to admit it – in reality, my faith for finances had never been in God. It had been in my wage packet, in the organization I had chosen to work for, in my CV or in my own limited abilities. Yet when I considered my second-rate (2:2) degree, from an average university, won by colouring in maps and talking about mountains, and compared it with choosing faith in the almighty God who built those resplendently beautiful contours while owning the cattle on those thousand colourful hills, I came to see that faith in God rather than in myself was, on balance, a better idea. Easy when you put it down on paper! A bit harder, for me at any rate, when you come to leaning back and actually falling into his arms.

I suppose you could say all this constitutes what Christians sometimes term 'a calling'. I have gone into how the process was for me, not because I am anything special, but because it most certainly wasn't clear, defined, exact or specific. Sometimes I meet people who can say, with an assurance lacking on my part, 'God called me here.' Sometimes they drop it into the middle of a sentence without pausing for breath. I never know quite how to react to that – but usually it makes me want to ask more questions, such as 'How do you know he did?'

Personally, I tend to avoid statements like 'He called me' – or if I do use such language, I feel the need to qualify it a bit by referring to the small steps that inched me forward. Not faith steps, but doubt steps. Tiny steps. Every one of them riddled and bedevilled with fear and hesitation.

I would add one further point I learned: if you are in a phase where you are thinking of stepping out to start a charity or feel God calling you to something new, be careful whose advice you listen to. Please assess risks and plan thoroughly, but also remember that sometimes good people, who want good for you, can give good reasons for you not to do good. Those reasons might need to be ignored. Faith is fundamentally about action and risk. You will need to take some actions and some risks somewhere on your faith journey – although it isn't that risky once you realize you are leaning into the arms of the all-powerful God who is calling you.

11

The first home opens

Vision without action is a daydream. Action without vision is a nightmare.

–Japanese proverb

After all these stepping stones of guidance, prayer, waiting and inching forward, it was time to actually turn the idea into reality. It was time to get out of the boat.

The success of the whole plan hinged not only on finding money, a mortgage, a house and some tenants, but also on finding a group of people crazy enough to support my wild idea by befriending the tenants. Whom could I pick on for such a role? David, my minister, decided we should target a homegroup from our church.

I had spoken numerous times to groups of people and rarely, if ever, felt nervous. However, as I sat in a room with ten people I already knew, I was more nervous than I had ever been. If they said no, the whole plan was dead. All my thinking and praying would come to nothing.

Fortunately, however, the group was made up of some amazing people, and they responded enthusiastically. A founding member of the church, Chris Campling, boundless in energy and constant in service, was quick to pitch in: 'We know there's a prison there, Ed, and we know we should do something to help prisoners, but we don't always know what to do.'

The next stepping stone had been crossed. Now we could launch out into the tangible business of finding a house. Our savings were insufficient to buy a property outright, so the only way we could make it happen was to take out a mortgage. Buying a house for an ex-offender is an unnatural thing to do, and I was certainly anxious about it. Fortunately, Rach was completely supportive of the crazy notion to pour all our savings and a substantial mortgage into this wild plan. She was amazing throughout the whole process, listening to all my thoughts and anxieties, always backing me in my pursuit of my unconventional scheme and never begrudging the time I was spending on it.

We started looking for houses and, after a few viewings, found one that was perfect. It was just a five-minute walk from the church and near a nice park – and had the important advantage of not being in 'drug dealers' alley'. It had three bedrooms, a downstairs lounge, a decent kitchen and was within our price range (just). It was the type of house I would be happy for my daughter to rent when she got older.

We had reached the next stepping stone. We put in our offer.

At around this time, Andy got in touch with me to suggest I meet up with one of the officers from the prison. I had no idea why, but I dutifully followed instructions. I shot off an email to the officer and soon we were sitting having a drink in a supermarket café in Bretton. He was a 'salt of the earth' kind of guy, typical of the level-headed unsung heroes of the criminal justice system that prison officers so often are. Although he was not a Christian, and had no interest in becoming one, he could understand the value of what I was trying to do with the churches. He had seen so many prisoners leave with nowhere to go – only to boomerang back after a few months – and he desperately wanted to help. After we had chatted for a while, I suddenly saw the penny drop and out came the words: 'Oh, I know a prisoner you need to meet. His name is Carlos. He's become a part of the Christian community in prison and has done a course in theology while he's been inside. Perhaps you could help him.'

I went home and looked Carlos up on the internet. He had clearly carried out some pretty impressive fraud. His case had been in the newspaper of the town he came from, and the photo of him walking to court revealed a handsome man, smartly dressed in an expensive suit.

In no time, I was having my fingerprint scanned at the prison gate and then walking through the massive electric doors, wondering what on earth I was doing. I had never done anything like this or been involved in the life of a prisoner before.

Carlos was now dressed in prison overalls. As we sat together, he told me his story and shared how his 'high life' and materialism had led him down the wrong paths into some very bad decisions. He was now at the absolute bottom of the heap. He had no money at all, no degree or qualifications to speak of, and no idea what he would do to earn a living. His marriage had fallen apart, he had lost virtually all his friends, his mother lived abroad, his father had passed away and he had absolutely nowhere to go on release. The atmosphere was electric as I realized this house I was buying might actually meet a genuine need, and he realized I might be the answer to his desperate prayers.

I walked out of the prison elated at the thought that my vision might finally be materializing. 'Could this crazy plan actually work?' I asked myself with excitement. At the same time, my mind reeled with anxiety at the idea that I might really be about to house a former convict.

Shortly after this, I met up with James, the young man who had found Peter Sullins' body. We sat together on the grass outside Bretton shopping centre as he told me about the harrowing experience of the discovery. He described how he had had an instinct that something might have gone wrong for Peter, and had gone to his room and found him dead. I could see that the trauma of the incident, now over 18 months ago, was still haunting him. After we had spoken for a while, I asked him about his living situation, and he told me he had been staying in hostels for over five years. He explained that he was recovering from an addiction and had no other housing options open to him. He felt trapped in the system.

I told him about the house I was buying and then asked him if he would like to live there. He looked at me to check he was hearing correctly. Then, as he took in the reality of the offer, his eyes lit up, and his face flooded with relief and excitement. He couldn't quite believe I was actually offering him a real home to live in; his answer was yes.

In the meantime, our purchase had been moving forward and we were now the owners of the property. There was plenty to do. Although it was a nice house, it needed quite a bit of work to get it up to a good standard. A new kitchen, a change of carpets and a good lick of paint throughout were all on the list. I thus began a frustrating process of engaging in negotiations, dealing with under-delivery and coping with overcharging, courtesy of a range of contractors.

Aside from wrangling with the workers, I was investing my fair share of effort in the renovations, alongside doing my full-time job. As I was there in the early hours of the morning, painting the rooms, I came to see the difference between grace and compassion. Compassion comes naturally to the human heart: you see a child starving, and you have compassion for him or her. However, when it's after midnight and you are painting a room for some bloke who has clearly done a crime and deserves to be behind bars, then you may not necessarily feel compassion. Instead you are beginning to understand grace.

After about a month of working on the house, we were nearly there. The carpets looked great, the kitchen was in and the paint was dry. Rach had taken care of all sorts of details – things I would never have thought of – that had turned the house into a future home. The church support group had thoughtfully bought groceries and chocolates to welcome the tenants.

Just before James and Carlos were due to move in, we met at the house to pray. It was exciting for me as I sensed, for the first time, that others were beginning to understand the vision. After we had prayed, someone privately offered £500. I nearly fell off my chair. We could now afford a washing machine. I'll never forget that gift!

While it was a fairly standard prayer meeting for the others, for me, inwardly, it was one of the biggest spiritual buzzes I have ever experienced. I couldn't sleep that night; I just lay there praising God. For weeks and months I had stepped out, invested all our savings in a house, done it up, argued with the builders refurbishing it, been stung by the cost of the electricity bill, and wondered time and again, over and over, if I was going mad. When others finally 'got' what I was doing, I felt awash with joy.

The next day, the dream became a reality: James moved into the house. Although he was desperate to leave the hostel, he was also anxious about moving. However, all went well, and we saw an almost immediate benefit to his health, with his sleep, diet and weight all improving.

Meanwhile, Carlos was still in prison. In order for him to be released, we needed, so the official letter told me, to go to a court with said prisoner and offer a 'surety' for his release. This was a complete shock to me. No one had told me about this process, and it was not what I'd understood normally happened. Besides which, when I received the letter, I had no idea what on earth 'surety' meant. I phoned up a lawyer friend who explained that if the former prisoner absconded or broke the terms of his probation, I would be the one who paid the 'surety'.

Good grief.

'How much would be wise to put up?'

'Don't go above four hundred pounds.'

'Got it.'

On the day of the hearing, I turned up early at court and sat in the waiting room, working on my laptop. The battery went dead. I had nothing left to do but stare at the walls, so I sat there and prayed. My thoughts turned to the inner workings of the cow's digestive system. This was not as random as it sounds. The day before, our minister, David, had been describing how cows use their four stomachs to redigest their food four times. By the end of the process, they have done a pretty good job of absorbing what they have taken in. I put the same principle into practice with ruminating on Scripture, repeatedly quoting the text of Psalm 68.6: 'God sets the lonely in families, he leads out the prisoners with singing'.

Eventually I was called to go into the hearing. It was my first time in an English court.

A stern judge presided at the end of a long room, on an elevated platform. I was told, in no uncertain terms, to sit at the back. His voice rippled with authority. All power in the room was with him. Officers stood guard; the prisoner sat between me and the judge, and all I could see of him was the back of his head. When the judge asked me to explain my relationship, I replied timidly, 'I've bought a house for this man; we've met twice and I'm keen to support his reintegration into society.'

A long silence as the judge looked down at his papers. I hadn't felt like this since being summoned to the headteacher's office.

Eventually the reply came: 'Can you show evidence of two thousand pounds for the surety?'

'How much?' I heard myself whimper in a high-pitched voice.

Our savings account was down to just a few hundred pounds as we had ploughed virtually everything into the house. Thankfully, I had been paid only days before, so, between my recently topped-up current account and my depleted savings account, I could just provide evidence of £2,000.

'I have it between two of my bank accounts, but I haven't brought any statements. However, I could show you online. But I would have to go back to the car to get my laptop – and I think the battery's dead.'

The court held its breath. The judge paused, bit his top lip in annoyance and then nodded. An officer, evidently understanding the instruction, ordered me out and accompanied me to my car. Miraculously, the laptop found a bit more juice and linked to the internet on my smartphone. I managed to get just enough power to show the officer my two accounts online. He squinted at my sun-drenched screen as he slowly examined my statements. We returned to court. Release was granted for two days' time.

I went to the car and began the drive home.

'Flippin' 'eck, God,' I moaned, 'I know I've said I would give or share anything for you, but this is a bit closer to the wire than I'd envisaged.'

On a serious note, I wouldn't advise anyone else to do this.

Two days after my experience at court, I went to meet Carlos at the prison gate. Standing waiting alongside me was another man, and we struck up an awkward conversation. As the first prisoners to be released started coming through the gates, I realized why he was there: he was waiting to push drugs to the men at their first breath of freedom.

Carlos was last out, and he greeted me with a warm smile as he came through the gates. He then went to collect his only personal possession from the reception area: one watch. I drove him to the house. It was an unusual experience for both of us. Although he was naturally a composed character, I could see Carlos was a bit off balance at the intensity of life on the outside. He hadn't seen cars for 18 months and was scared by the speed at which everything was moving. I read later that after the lack of stimulation in jail, it can be shocking and tiring for prisoners to process the world around them on release; apparently, they make roughly 2,000 decisions a day in prison, while those on the outside make around 10–15,000 in the same time frame.

After the intensity of the journey, I think Carlos was even more grateful to have a home he could retreat into.

The next Sunday I went to our church as usual and was overjoyed to see both James and Carlos already there. We had mentioned the church but had not put any pressure on them to attend. It was a major spiritual buzz for me to know they had come to the service.

I continued building a relationship with James and Carlos. I met them regularly and helped them with the next stages of their lives. They would come over to our home and eat with us from time to time, and Rach and I would sometimes go to their home and do a Bible study with them.

About one month after they had moved in, Carlos came to me with a major need. I researched it and felt it was credible, worthy and valuable. Up until now in my career, I had always been able to find some funds when I met a genuine need. Not so in this fledgling charity. Hope into Action now had a bank account, but it literally had no money in it at all. (My personal account was the same.) The next day, I got up and prayed hard into the situation before I headed off to work. I hadn't mentioned the need to Rach, but when I got home she told me she had bumped into someone who had happened to drop into the conversation that she was on the board of a small trust fund. The board members happened to be meeting the next week. So a quick phone call, a rushed proposal, and within ten days of my prayer we had received just over £1,000 to meet the need. God was teaching me about dependence on him and revealing how he shows mercy to the righteous and the unrighteous alike.

Both Carlos and James were to become major parts of my life and story.

James remains a friend to this day. He and I recently cycled 50 miles to Lincoln on a sponsored bike ride, as he wanted to raise money for Hope into Action.

Carlos never broke his probation conditions, and I remained solvent. He ended up volunteering, and then working, for us for a few years, and we became close friends. For reasons I cannot share, his relationship with us later broke down. He had done so much good for Hope into Action, but I, together with others, was left feeling hurt by him. After I was faced with no choice other than to sack him, he no doubt felt hurt by me too.

The whole process of buying the house, involving the church, finding and bringing in the tenants – and waiting to see if housing benefit would cover the rent – was one of the most nerve-racking experiences of my life. But it had happened! The vision had become a reality.

12

He broke the loaves

Taking the five loaves and the two fish and looking up to
heaven, he gave thanks and broke the loaves.

–Matthew 14.19

I was buzzing with excitement that the first house seemed to be
going well. Not much later we were an official charity, complete
with a charity number. But where did we go from there? I knew
God intended Hope into Action to be about more than one home,
but I had no idea where more houses would come from. I reckoned
there was money out there in the form of grants, so I spent my
early morning hours churning out grant applications. The days and
weeks passed and virtually nothing trickled in. I was gutted. Cash
was vital for us to be able to run. I felt stuck.

In the autumn of 2010 the UK's Coalition Government had
announced its budget cuts, leaving the entire voluntary sector and
local councils reeling as they came to terms with a very different
financial outlook. Services and projects were slashed or ended
altogether. In Peterborough the cuts led to four homeless charities
going bust over the next few years. It was an inauspicious time to
start a charity, let alone grow one. After the autumn budget I felt
totally flat, not to mention anxious. My anxiety drove me to read
the minute details of the Government's plans to work out how they
would affect us. Yet I held on to my trust that the God I believed in
was bigger than our government and even our economy.

Out of the blue, I received an email from a woman called Karen
at the city council. She mentioned she had heard about what we
were doing and asked me to come to her office for a chat. Feeling

quite intimidated, I went to meet her and shared the goals of our project with her. In the light of the climate of cynicism about faith-based work, I was expecting her to give me a hard time. She fired question after question at me, most of which left me feeling out of my depth. I tried to emphasize the involvement of my church, and the relationships being built between the homegroup members and the tenants.

A few months later, in January 2011, Karen invited me back. A burly bloke, high up in the management of the local prison, joined us. Karen opened up by saying, 'Ed, I'm not a Christian, don't believe in God and don't go to church, but I can't find the kind of social capital you're talking about anywhere in the city, so I've found some money, forty-four thousand pounds, and I wonder if you could use it to help buy a house?'

I thought about it and, magnanimously, agreed to accept her offer.

'Good. I'm glad to hear it, because I've also persuaded the prison to give you thirty-three thousand pounds for another house. Could you buy a house with that as well?'

I thought about it and, magnanimously, agreed to accept that offer also.

'Great. I'll write the proposal for the council money. Please send an invoice to the prison for thirty-three thousand pounds.'

Something about the spirit of the new year must have got to me because, once again, I agreed.

After the meeting I scurried home and phoned up Gavin Bateman, our chair of trustees.

'Gavin, do you know how to prepare an invoice?'

Thankfully, he did. It was the best invoice I have ever seen.

It is hard to overemphasize how unusual this is. We were a charity with only one house, no track record and no accounts. We didn't even have to write a proposal. Years later, people have looked at our financial accounts (which are stored publicly online) and seen some money from a prison in there and asked me about it. One man put it like this: 'Ed, I've been trying to get money out of our local prison for years; they've not even given us two hundred pounds. How on earth did you manage to get thirty-three thousand?'

The first bit of multiplied bread.[1]

After I had got my head around the invoice, I needed to find churches to partner with us in running the houses. I raced here and there, trying to persuade church leaders; thankfully, I found two who were willing to partner with us.

The first church, Open Door Church, was led by a great couple called Maggie and Russ. Maggie had spent much of her life caring for people who had known rejection. When I went to their home, I discovered they were housing a 21-year-old former prostitute. I liked and admired Maggie and Russ for their faith and warm interest in people. As we looked into our options, we realized their church was in an area where the price of houses exceeded what we thought we could afford. However, we prayed about it with the church leaders and thought we would give it a try. The day after we had prayed, we received a call from the estate agent: 'There's a house that has been repossessed. The lender is selling it at a knock-down price – do you want it?'

We went to look at the house and discovered it was just round the corner from the church community centre and opposite a park. You bet we wanted it.

We managed to negotiate a price at around £20,000 below market value. Just one small thing remained: a mortgage.

I tried Charity Bank, Kingdom Bank and every other kind of bank I could find. None would lend to a charity unless it had at least three years' worth of published accounts. We had been registered for just over five months at this point. I'd got us into a corner, and I realized that if God didn't bother turning up, we'd be stuffed.

Not knowing what to do next, I phoned up Yvonne, our trustee who had expertise in housing. Rather than give me the rollicking

I deserved for foolishly rushing ahead and getting us into a tight spot, she picked up her nearest weapon, jumped into the trench right alongside me and just started firing. Her tenacity in trying to find a solution was something to behold, and I knew then that I would always want to go into battle with this woman. However, not even Yvonne could find a solution: we were at the end of our options. If this house fell through, we would have to hand all the money back. Surely God did not want us to do that? Our only recourse was prayer, and our only action was to wait and see what God would do.

While I was waiting to see what would happen, the next provision was to really take me by surprise.

13

Tragedy and redemption

Lord, make me an instrument of thy peace; where there is
hatred, let me sow love . . . where there is despair, hope.

–The Prayer of St Francis

'I've spent the last thirty years serving with the police force. I thoroughly enjoyed it and now I'm retiring. I quite like the idea of using some of my retirement lump-sum cash to buy a house to be used for ex-offenders. Are you interested?'

If I've ever felt my jaw drop at the hinges and my eyeballs pop out like a silly cartoon character, then this was it. When Steve had asked at church if he could pop over to see Rach and me, I certainly hadn't seen it coming.

Steve had been stationed with the local police when the London bombing now known as '7/7' happened. Among the 50 victims who had died in that attack was a young man called James Adams who was part of our church. Steve had been there to support the family, protect them from the media, and help them and the church through their grief. James had left his house to his parents, Ernie and Elaine, who had held on to it in an empty state. Steve proposed to them that he would buy the house from them, at market value, and use it for Hope into Action. James had always had a heart for the homeless and had worked at nearby Whitemoor prison for a short while. This proposal, five years after his death, sat warmly with his parents. As Ernie proudly showed Steve around the house, he opened the dishwasher and found, for the first time, some of James's cutlery still there. The sight of the utensils brought back some pain, and Ernie stopped talking, stood by the dishwasher and wept.

As the sale proceeded quickly and there was not much work to be done on the house, this turned out to be our second Hope into Action home.

It was a special moment as we gathered to pray before our first tenant, Thomas, moved in. Thomas was an ex-offender, and it was a joy to see James's house being used for Steve's vision to give offenders a better chance as they moved on.

Elaine mentioned several times how the launch of the house had lifted a huge burden from Ernie. He died within a year of the house opening, but he did so with a lighter heart.

Elaine still worships at our church and is a source of unending encouragement and positivity for us.

It was a poignant experience to be involved with an ex-cop buying a house for ex-offenders, redeeming a property that previously stood as a reminder of a tragic killing, and using it to bring life and hope to others.

The house reflected the two ends of the spectrum of tragedy and redemption. Later, I would encounter the two ends of the social spectrum at the same location, hosting one of the most powerful men in the UK and housing one of the least acknowledged in the country: one flanked by the media, the other shunned by even his own family. While the first came with anticipation and excitement, it was the second that changed me.

14

White-knuckle ride

Faith by itself, if it is not accompanied by action, is dead.

–James 2.17

While Steve's house had been moving forward, we still had our bid in on the house we wanted to buy with the council's money, but we just could not raise a mortgage. The thought of having to admit defeat and hand back the funds was awful. Money like that comes along very rarely. I kept trying different banks of all shapes and sizes. They all said they wouldn't give a mortgage without at least some accounts having been filed.

Being unable to see a solution and having no sense of control are a perfect recipe for stress, and that recipe was certainly working for me. The lack of a way forward, together with the fear that I would have to hand back £44,000 and £33,000 to the council and prison respectively, was occupying my thoughts last thing at night and first thing in the morning.

Then, out of the blue, Yvonne told me she had heard some news: quite unexpectedly the Government had opened a loophole that allowed start-up companies to get a mortgage. She hatched a plan. Within the space of a few days, she and I became directors of a company, Kayak Properties. We checked whether the council would be okay with transferring the money to the company, and the officials were happy with the arrangement. We were able to get a mortgage for the company that covered the cost of the property and the refurbishment. I asked the prison authorities if they would also be in agreement with this arrangement, and they too were happy, so we soon had two more properties in the pipeline.

Amazingly, shortly after we completed our purchase of the second of these two properties, the Government closed the loophole and it was no longer possible to get a mortgage as a start-up company. It was almost as if the sea had parted, and we had walked straight through and then watched it close behind us once safe on the other side.[1] This journey of faith is sleep-depriving, adrenalin-pumping, highly risky, white-knuckle stuff!

15

A key to a new home

Never worry about numbers. Help one person at a time and
always start with the person nearest you.

–Mother Teresa

After our first home had opened, I met up with Gavin Howard and
asked him whether he would be willing to consider buying a house
to lease to Hope into Action. He agreed to discuss the idea with
his wife, Lucinda, and amazingly they said yes. To this day, I am
deeply grateful that they were quick to invest from the outset in
this potentially hair-brained scheme. Gavin is perhaps one of the
purest-hearted people I know, with a great brain and lovely presence to boot.

From time to time I would meet up with Graham Timson,
the father of Phil, the evangelist who had called me forward to
prophesy over me. Graham, like his son, always seemed to wear
an encouraging smile and had a heart for those in need. We would
get together at Phil's house or to play the odd game of golf, and he
was forever open to hearing what I was up to. I was also interested
in his activities; he ran a charity for overseas work in developing
countries, and on Sunday nights he led a service for the homeless.
He knew many of the Peterborough homeless by name, and they in
turn knew him. When Gavin agreed to buy a house, Graham's was
the first door I went to knock on. He and his church, named Church
on the Rock (now City Church), agreed in no time to partner with
us. We began looking for a house and found one literally a stone's
throw away from his church. We put in an offer and we were on
our way.

While the house was being made ready, Graham recommended that we meet and assess two men whom he had known for a while, Paul and Scotty. Both had done the rounds in Peterborough. Both had had a long-term relationship with heroin but were now on methadone (a heroin substitute issued as a blocker to those in recovery from addiction). Both were sleeping rough.

Within a month of our second home opening, we had our third property. Once the purchase was completed, I was desperate to get Paul and Scotty into the house at the very first opportunity. Neither of them had a mobile phone, so I found myself getting up at the crack of dawn the next day and running up and down the riverbank where they slept. Eventually, somewhat breathless, I found them and told them the good news that they and their dog now had a new home. However, moving them in turned out to be more of a palaver than I had anticipated. Despite being homeless and living in a tent, they had loads of stuff. It was just all stored at different people's houses.

Such was my early zeal and sense of urgency to get these two men housed that I didn't really think through all that we were meant to do. We should have seen to it that we had gas safety and electrical certificates. Now we do all these things properly, but at that moment all I could think of was preventing them from spending another night out on the riverbank.

Paul and Scotty made interesting housemates, with contrasting characters and personalities. Paul would charm us all; Scotty was shy, and chats with him rarely lasted more than two sentences. Paul was well dressed and used to dominate conversations; Scotty was slovenly and would sometimes bend over when talking as if in a position of submission. Paul was obsessively tidy and would constantly clean and improve the house; Scotty was often very unorganized. Scotty had six daughters. He told me how his partner had been abusive towards him – and then added, 'So I went out to get a dog . . . and what d'ya know? She was a bitch too.'

As I moved them in, I stopped to take a photo of them holding the key to their new home. Somehow that picture captured so much of what I wanted us to stand for: empowering people with trust, a key and a new home, with smiles of hope and happiness plastered over their gnarled and weathered faces.

The joy of that moment was to be part of a rollercoaster ride with challenges and heartbreak – and further moments of joy – along its path. Despite all the ups and downs that lay ahead, I wouldn't have missed out on being a part of it.

16

The father of all rollickings

I will instruct you and teach you in the way you should go; I
will counsel you and watch over you.

–Psalm 32.8 NIV 1984

With the initial houses open, it was a struggle for me to keep up
with all the demands of managing the properties and running the
charity while also working full time. It was getting to the stage
where I just could not do justice to all that was involved in the hours
I had in my evenings, lunch breaks and weekends.

I remember one morning when this was all too apparent, as I
juggled my responsibilities while worrying over an issue I felt ill-
equipped to handle at Hope into Action.

Rach was away at work, and I was on parent duty, in charge of
getting my girls to school and nursery. It wasn't going well. We
should have left five minutes earlier. For the previous ten minutes
I had been failing to persuade one of my daughters to get dressed,
and she was currently as far away from her bedroom as it was physically possible to be without leaving the house.

I was about to blow my top in an unseemly way and give both my
daughters the father of all rollickings. Just as I was about to erupt,
I realized that doing so would only lead to tears and even further
delays to our ever-receding departure time.

Instead, I retreated into my bedroom, grabbed my Bible, sank to
my knees, opened the Psalms and tried to focus. The first text I fell
on was from Psalm 32: 'I will instruct you and teach you in the way
you should go; I will counsel you and watch over you.'[1]

I paused and reread, then paused and reread again and again.

After a few more quiet minutes, I got up and found my daughter dressed and ready to go. I felt a calm that would have been almost impossible to imagine five minutes previously, and we all skipped off to school. Our late arrival did not result in the sky falling in.

I can't remember now what the issue was that I was worrying about; that probably means it got resolved. I do know, however, that this was a moment when I felt a peace that transcended understanding. I knew then that whatever came before us, God would provide someone who knew something about the issue to guide us. I had a strong sense that God would direct our steps, just as Jesus had directed the steps of the disciples in the feeding of the 5,000 – even regarding the size of groups they should get the people to sit in.[2]

This is exactly what happened. When I needed to know something about benefits, I bumped into a benefits consultant who explained it to me in a way I could understand; when we needed to know more about governance, someone suggested a really helpful book; when we were thinking about a new website, someone pointed us to some funding for an expert website designer; when we needed to understand franchising, we met Mark Kitson, who had previously overseen franchising for a major UK coffeehouse chain, and on the list goes.

As I look back, I see the words given to me at the start of the journey being fulfilled: 'Whether you turn to the right or to the left, your ears will hear a voice behind you, saying, "This is the way; walk in it."'[3]

None of this means that we haven't made mistakes, that we always agree or that we never do things without sin (and it certainly doesn't mean I have never been stressed since – just ask my daughters). However, it does mean that there is a trust at the core of our organization – a belief that God is directing us. I hope this book is a testament, not to our skills (though we are constantly trying to develop and hone these), but to his provision and direction.

17

The big step

Can we unmask our deeper need for love and relationship in lieu of power, money, things and success?

–*Shane Claiborne*, The Irresistible Revolution, *2007*

By early summer 2011, even though I had made progress in being more at peace, the demands were still intense, and I was increasingly aware it wasn't possible to fit running Hope into Action into my spare time. The trustees could also see that for Hope into Action to continue and for the vision to grow, I would need to invest all my working hours in it. We all felt that the right solution would be for me to go full time. The only problem was that the financial situation did not look favourable: hardly any money in Hope into Action's bank account, no major donor or church behind us, and Rach and I supporting a mortgage and the voracious appetites of our two children (although less voracious when it came to vegetables).

We came together for a trustees' meeting at my home. I could sense the trustees were feeling more on edge than usual, with responsibility for the next step weighing on them. Yet there was also an air of faith-filled confidence in God. After some pretty lively prayer, heartfelt seeking after God, and then discussion, we came to the decision that we would step out in faith: I would work full time for Hope into Action and would receive a salary 20 per cent below my current income.

The chair, Gavin Bateman, looked a bit more relaxed now and suggested we close the meeting in prayer. At this point Rach, sitting next to me, nudged me under the table, and I knew she wanted me to say something.

'Oh,' I said, 'one more thing I should tell you. Rach is pregnant.'

Silence. (You might say a 'pregnant silence'.)

Andy's jaw dropped to the floor as his eyes popped out of his head. He looked at me as if to say '*What?* You total idiots. How are you going to afford that?'

The awkwardness was diffused by Gavin. Years of protocol in Her Majesty's Services equipped him with the correct response: 'What wonderful news. When is the baby due?'

With the decision made, I gave my three months' notice at my work and prepared for a big change in my life.

As I was getting ready to go full time, our support staff was starting to grow, with a (very) part-time administrative staff member coming on board and one of our former tenants volunteering to provide support to our current residents; after he had been with us for 18 months we gave him some responsibility, and he proved good at his role.

There were new concerns. Where would I be based? With a new baby on the way, working from home certainly didn't seem an ideal option. With our new staff members, we even more certainly could not all cram into our house. However, neither would it have been ideal if we were spread out across the city working in separate locations. We really needed an office space, but there was no money to finance this.

Several months earlier, Gavin Howard had alerted me to a group of Christians dealing in property. I had gone to see the patron, Colin Molyneux, in his swanky office in Bond Street in the centre of London. We had had an interesting conversation, but nothing much had come from it.

Just as we were realizing we needed an office, I received an email from Colin. By 'coincidence', he was doing some business in Peterborough and happened to have some spare office space; were we interested? Yes, we were *very* interested! We met for a coffee in town, and he took me round an office on the third floor of a block located less than 200 yards from the cathedral.

Thus, on 1 August 2011, the day I started working full time for Hope into Action, I was able to walk straight into a newly repainted office suite in the heart of Peterborough. Furnished with desk and chairs. Rent free.

The provision continued over the years to come. As our staff increased, we were able to move to a larger office on a floor below. Still rent free.

18

Mothers

While they were there, the time came for her baby to be born.
She gave birth to her firstborn son. She wrapped him snugly
in strips of cloth and laid him in a manger, because there was
no lodging available for them.

–Luke 2.6–7 NLT

Shortly after I resigned from my job, we were able to buy our fourth
house with the money from the council and the mortgage through
Kayak Properties. The crew at Open Door Church did an amazing
job of refurbishing the property and turning it into a home for the
first tenants. Maggie knew a man called Kelvin, who was homeless
and feeling down for a variety of reasons. She took him for a walk
one day and deliberately steered their route past the house. As they
walked past, she interrupted him to ask, 'Kelvin, how would you
like to live in a house like this?' She told him about the scheme
and then offered him a room. By the time she had finished talking,
Kelvin was in tears. He couldn't believe anyone would do such a
thing for him.

I was convinced that God had moved miraculously for us to
get both the funding and the house. I thought all I would have to
do now was put some guys in, and God's miraculous work would
continue: addictions would end overnight, healings would occur,
faith would rise and the Church would grow. Well, there has been
some of that, but I have come to realize that transformation and
healing are a lot harder to attain than I expected.

What I also didn't anticipate at the time was that this would be
the very spot at which my life would be threatened.

The home was for two people, so we had a space available for a housemate for Kelvin. A referral came through, but it was for a couple. The report revealed that both the guy, Pat, and the woman, Sian, battled with addiction to heroin. Pat had committed some drug-related crimes and Sian had got caught up in one of them, and they had both done some time as a result. Sian was now six months pregnant and homeless. Although we had the vacancy, I felt there was no way we should take them because I was sure the council would find them a place. Six weeks later they were referred back to us, still homeless, and now she was seven and a half months pregnant. What should I do? I thought of the innkeeper who slammed the door on a homeless pregnant woman and missed out on meeting the living Christ. I didn't want to be guilty of the same sin; I decided to welcome them into the house.

Although Pat had a criminal record as long as your arm, and Sian's wasn't the shortest either, they made the house look really cosy, and he worked hard to get the garden into good shape. However, it wasn't long before he was up before the courts again and sent down for some further time for an old crime that had caught up with him. The day after he was sentenced, Sian went into labour and gave birth to a beautiful baby daughter.

The church members did an excellent job of taking care of Sian and her child, both before and after the baby was born, popping in to look after them and helping with food and clothing and other needs. I visited Sian a few days after the birth and asked her, 'Is there anything you would like me to do for you?' (This was a paraphrase of a question Jesus had once asked that I had been thinking about.[1])

She replied that she got really nervous leaving the baby asleep when she had to go downstairs to the kitchen. 'Could you possibly get a monitor?' she asked shyly.

We had just been given some money, and I wanted to try to reflect God's generous heart towards her, so I bought one of the best baby monitors available and hoped it would give a glimmer of God's love for her. As I handed it to her, her eyes grew big, and she thanked me in a croaky voice with such heartfelt gratitude that I will never forget it.

Since Sian moved in with us, we have opened many homes for women. Naturally, working with women will involve working with children at times. In addition, given the circumstances of many of our tenants' lives, social services can also be part of the dynamic. There is often a real concern among our tenants that they may lose their child or children to social services. They know how the care system works, how it feels, how it smells; they have been there; their family members' children have been there; they really don't want their own kids there.

In Sian's case, we were able to work with social services and the church to enable her and her baby to stay together. Since then, we have been able to help a number of other mothers to keep their children.

However, this was not always the case, as I was to experience in perhaps the most baffling and disempowering experience of all my work with Hope into Action.

19

'For the first time in my life I felt like I was worth something'

A cold, self-righteous prig who goes regularly to church may be far nearer to hell than a prostitute.

–*C. S. Lewis*

Not long after we had bought our fourth house, we were able to buy a fifth house with the finances from the prison and the mortgage we had got through the amazing loophole that had opened up.

So, within the space of a few months, we had opened our second, third, fourth and fifth houses.

When the mortgage for the fifth house came through, I immediately thought of Kingsgate Church in Peterborough. I had known the person in charge of its social action work, Juliet Welch, for some time and had always appreciated her heart and all the church was doing. I called her up, and she was immediately keen to be involved and said she would talk the idea through with the church leaders. They came back to say they would like to partner with the house, and that they had a vision for it to be an all-female home. We were very pleased with the proposal and were quick to agree.

Our first tenant was a woman I will call Lyndsey, who came directly from prison. However, I found I needed to limit my involvement in helping her, because on my first visit her hand kept 'accidentally' straying on to my backside. Once she moved on, I felt a bit more comfortable about visiting the house, alongside another member of staff, and I met our new tenant, Sally.

Sally was a delightful, vivacious lady, very engaging and a good conversationalist. She had black hair framing a face that seemed naturally inclined to smile. Her jolly demeanour betrayed no hint of her challenges or her battles with co-dependency and depression. The difficulties she faced were intense, but she has made such great progress. She describes her journey in the following words:

My mum was a single parent. Things started to go very wrong for me when she met a new partner, who became more and more physically, mentally and sexually abusive towards me. Mum chucked me out of the house when I was a teenager, so I stayed with another family on the estate. But I was in a horrific house fire there.

At about 14, I was put into care, but I was abused again at the children's care home. I began to use drink and drugs as a way to escape the pain, and I did anything I could to survive.

Over the next few years I had two daughters and two sons, but they were adopted together into another family as I wasn't in a fit state to be the mother they needed me to be. I continued to self-medicate with alcohol and drugs and ended up suffering several nervous breakdowns, before being diagnosed with bipolar disorder. I managed to get clean for a few years, but then fell back into drugs and prostitution.

Throughout my life, I've been hurt and manipulated by people whom I should have been able to trust – people who should have cared for me and kept me safe. I've wanted to die on more than one occasion and would often go to bed not caring whether I woke up the next day or not.

Having been right at the very bottom, I'm now scraping my way back up. I remember pleading with my doctor saying, 'I need some divine intervention right now as I'm homeless again.' She told me about Hope into Action and the way they help people like me. I had two meetings to explore the possibility of moving into one of their houses. I nearly didn't move in, but I am *so* glad I did! Looking back, it really feels like it was meant to be.

At first, I relapsed a lot, but after a particularly bad episode when I almost died, I have been able to stay off drugs. The people from Hope into Action were bothering with me; for the first time in my life, I felt like I was worth something. Now I cherish every day as a blessing. Just eight weeks after moving into the house, one of my daughters got back in touch with me and I found out that I was a grandma! Things are definitely looking up for me. Hope into Action has given me the stability to regain what was stolen from me; I'm rebuilding relationships with my children and getting to know my grand-children, and I've made some amazing friends at church. I still have my ups and downs, of course, but my friends are my anchor; they keep me secure. I'm going to counselling now, and I love it. It's true what they say: life begins at 40! I've done an Alpha Course, moved on and given two talks at Hope into Action conferences.

I hope Sally's testimony highlights the fact that while a woman may be viewed as a 'prostitute' or a 'sex worker',[1] in reality she is a human first of all: a sister, a child, a daughter. No one is born a prostitute; something tragic has happened for a person to end up that way. (I know there are some who say it can be a choice, but all I can say is that for those we have met, this has never been the case: their 'choice' has been either abject misery or to 'work' to pay for a habit, childcare or something else. I've yet to meet a young girl who says that when she grows up she wants to be a 'prostitute'. Nor have I met a father of a young girl who states that his hopes and dreams are for his daughter to have a fulfilling career in sex work.) So Sally is not thought of as 'an addict', or 'a former prostitute': she is a charming, funny individual. I love her social media posts (one of which asked me, after the Windrush scandal, to sign a petition for Prime Minister Theresa May to be deported to the Caribbean), and it is a privilege to know her.

Each church selects 'befrienders' to support the tenants, and Sally's befriender, Heidi, made an instant connection with her. They were a good match in age and personality, and they got on fabulously. Heidi quickly invited Sally to her home, which really touched Sally and opened up a genuine friendship. Sally could see that for Heidi she was a real friend, not just a project. This was a unique experience for her, and a marked change from her interaction with others involved in helping her. It is these acts of love that make Hope into Action different, and this difference is felt by those we help. They can tell that we do not see them as clients. Sally and Heidi have become an ongoing and meaningful part of each other's lives.

When Heidi was asked to describe her experience of helping Sally, she shared these thoughts:

Sally is an inspiration to me. I've always been the Hope into Action volunteer with our church, but it hasn't always been a bed of roses when new tenants have come in. The people we support come from totally different walks of life. When you meet someone like Sally and find out what she's been through, you realize that they're often very strong people, and they can teach us a lot. The first time I met Sally was just after I'd been to the gym. Straight away she laughed at me – I wasn't in my 'Sunday best' and looked a right state! I immediately knew we'd get on. Sometimes I ask myself, 'Where does God want me to be?' I think my work with Hope into Action is a small part of where he wants me to be – but a very important one. I've also realized that it's just as much for my benefit as it is for the benefit of the people I support; it's incredibly humbling to be a part of someone's transformation. Seeing Sally transform her life and make new friendships has been a real blessing; I feel as if I've been watching her settle into her new nest, and now I'm really looking forward to seeing her flourish in the future, not just as her mentor, but as her friend.

There have been highs and lows along Sally's path since she joined us, including a mini-breakdown, but she remains our friend and speaks for us regularly. We have high hopes for her future.

20

'We want to show you how much you are worth'

Be merciful, just as your Father is merciful. Do not judge, and you will not be judged. Do not condemn, and you will not be condemned. Forgive, and you will be forgiven.

–Jesus in Luke 6.36–37

While we were getting the female house up and running in Peterborough, Gavin Howard was exploring a similar possibility in Cambridge. He was in touch with the pastor of C3 Church in Cambridge, Angie Campbell, who was already involved in any number of social projects. She shared with him that she had always dreamed of her church running a house for vulnerable women. Gavin brought the two of us together for a lunch to get the ball rolling and then found an investor. Things moved forward quickly, and we opened a women's house in Cambridge shortly after launching the one in Peterborough. Within less than a month of that one starting, we had a second female house open in Peterborough.

When I think of the women's house in Cambridge, I think of Susie, a young lass of mixed race, whom I helped move in on her first day with us. Susie was so lovely and so charming – and yet so broken at the same time. During the assessment phase, it was obvious that she desperately wanted to get a new home and make a new start. When she moved in, she was so touched by the quality of the house that she broke down in tears, saying, 'I can't believe you've done this for me. I don't believe I'm worth it.'

'Well,' came back the gentle reply from the church volunteer, 'we believe you are. We think you're amazing, and we want to show you how much you are worth.'

Susie did really well for a couple of months, before hooking up with her old partner. They shared a love of crack and cocaine, and he would pimp her out in order to score. In the end, her stealing got her into trouble and she returned to prison.

I remember cycling home one night crying out to God for Susie. She was clearly blessed with so much talent, charm and potential and yet could not seem to break free of addiction for more than six weeks. She had been through rehab but then returned to heroin; on more than one occasion she had got clean in prison, yet there was a relapse every time.

I saw her around a fair bit after she had finished her sentence, and she would always greet me with a smile. She popped into our Cambridge office one day and got chatting in her usual bubbly way.

'One of the staff told me you were pregnant, Susie?' I asked.

'Yes,' she replied. 'I terminated the pregnancy. Best thing I've ever done.'

She seemed so positive about it, and we carried on talking. Within about three minutes, however, it became clear that she was putting on a front – and that the front was quickly coming down. She told me she had two other children, who were both with her mum. Now she was beginning to wobble. Then she told me her brother had raped her when she was 13, and that her mother had never believed her. She was now so tearful that I did what most men do when confronted by an emotional female: panic. I called for Jill, an experienced worker who has dealt with every kind of situation before, and she came and took Susie into the counselling room.

An hour later, Jill came out of the room looking as though she had been hit by a bus. She had listened to every detail of the termination. Women with addictions are allowed to terminate their pregnancy later than normal law allows. Susie recounted how she had seen the aborted foetus/child with its fully formed arms, legs, fingers and toes, and had had a good enough view to recognize the gender. She felt devastated. She asked whether she had murdered her own son. Termination may be legal, safe and sanitized, but – whatever your views on it – it may be worth remembering the impact it can have on the mother (and father). The decision can haunt people for years – and with whom can they share their secret? Very often, sadly, it is a private grief they bury. For Susie, the rape 20 years ago was still haunting her, and, on top of that, she was now trying to deal with the emotions that came with a termination.

Our job in those circumstances is to love the individuals involved and show them kindness where they are. We try not to judge them. Sometimes that is difficult because our views and morals may not agree with their actions. It's at these times one realizes how hard it is to follow the teaching of Jesus: 'Be merciful, just as your Father is merciful. Do not judge, and you will not be judged. Do not condemn, and you will not be condemned. Forgive, and you will be forgiven.'[1]

21

It rips the heart out

Therefore, as God's chosen people, holy and dearly loved, clothe yourselves with compassion, kindness, humility, gentleness and patience.

–Colossians 3.12

Within 16 months of our first home opening, we were running seven houses, supported by churches from six different denominations. Jesus was multiplying those loaves all right.

I was preparing to go away for a couple of days for a much-needed break when Graham Timson came round to see me. He shared that he was worried about Scotty and showed me a picture of his room that had been taken during one of our standard inspections. In the midst of the chronic mess was a spoon with a brown stain on it. We thought about Scotty's behaviour over the past few weeks: not turning up to meetings, being unable to pay the rent, lying . . . These symptoms were new to me, and so close was I to him that I didn't want to believe the evidence. However, after chewing it over in a discussion, both Graham and I, with heavy hearts, concluded Scotty was back on heroin.

Heroin is such an evil drug. It's like a tyrant. It has a massive hold over people and is the root of so much destruction in their lives and relationships. It controls them, driving them to lie, steal, beg, prostitute and shame themselves in order to get one more hit. It forces them to place it above all else. It rips their heart out, controls their brain and crushes their soul. It retains a beautiful, horrible, alluring, evil, sweet, destructive power. And with 200,000 current users in the UK, it is ripping the heart and soul out of families and communities.

Even if a user manages to get on to methadone, he or she still needs to collect the prescribed dose from the chemist two or three times a week and so is effectively chained to the pharmacy.

Scotty had been on the streets for six years. His history was not great. When we had first got to know him, staff from the council had told us they had found him from time to time in the morning, lying in the gutter with a needle sticking out of his arm. They really didn't rate his chances of living long.

After we realized what was happening with Scotty, Graham and I tried to work out what we should do. We should really have evicted him, but we both felt it would be best to give him a final written warning.

I dropped the letter off with Scotty before going away on leave. His room stank, and I could see he was living in a disordered state. (I later came to recognize this as a telltale sign of relapse.) I explained to him that we liked him very much, but his behaviour was unacceptable, and if he was to stay in the house, his drug misuse had to stop.

I felt very emotionally engaged in his situation, and I prayed and prayed during my two-day break. While I was away, I went to hear a talk by Darrell Tunningley, a man who had been on drugs and in prison and was now leading a church. I bought the book of his testimony and left it at Scotty's place on my way home.

I carried on praying for Scotty, and remember a particularly intense time when I called on God with a deep sense of authority within the ancient prayer-soaked walls of Peterborough Cathedral. Graham and I both continued to stay in touch with him and monitor his situation.

A few weeks later, when I was out during a lunch break, I found Scotty begging in Peterborough city centre.

Once back in the office, I shared my concern with my colleagues. 'This isn't right,' I said with indignation. 'We cannot allow people to give him money while he's not homeless.'

I discussed the situation with the team and shared some thoughts I had been drawing together for an upcoming talk on Jesus and the adulterous woman. I suggested we should copy the order of ministry that Jesus had used in that encounter:

1 Minister through non-judgmental silence.
2 Prioritize the individual's needs – Jesus literally saved her life by putting his own on the line.
3 Once trust has been earned, engage in conversation and share the good news of God's love and forgiveness. As Jesus said to the woman caught in adultery: 'Neither do I [God] condemn you.'[1]
4 Only once the individual has understood the good news, provide advice.[2]

So often, we invert that order. We run around giving people advice months before we have earned the right to, with the result that they never listen to us.

We decided that we should follow this pattern that Jesus used in our dealings with Scotty. We would not judge, and we would have conversations with him.

I felt this was the right approach for Scotty. In our work with the homeless, we do need to balance grace with truth, and truth can involve challenge.

As we followed through the plan with him, the conversations occasionally even reached three or four sentences.

By the time Christmas came, we had found no further evidence of drug misuse in the house. We closed up the offices for the festive season, and on the first day back in the new year I heard the buzzer ring and Scotty's voice coming through on the intercom. I went down to open the door; he didn't come in and I don't think he even said hello; he just began to speak. (Have I told you he was also Scottish, with a thick accent? Even his two sentences of conversation were hard to decipher.) Here was this hardened street sleeper, whom we had nearly evicted, arriving at our door and, like a child running out of school with his latest drawing, proudly showing me the results of his drug test. He'd just been tested and was clean (though still on methadone).

Three months later I was delivering another letter to him – this time to congratulate him for being abstinent for over 12 weeks. He did have to remain on the methadone reduction programme, but nevertheless, for him to stay clean of heroin itself was a major achievement. Oh, and he stopped begging as well, even though we had never mentioned it.

Scotty got back in touch with his daughters; they would come and visit him, and he would cook for them. The following June, on my birthday, I had the joy of seeing Scotty being baptized. During the service, Psalm 40 was read, and never before had the words 'He lifted me out of the slimy pit' felt more apt.[3] It was a year after we had moved him in.

Fast forward a further six years, and one of his daughters is now raising money for us.

22

A mad and dangerous plan

My poor are sick because people speak about them but do not listen to them.

–*Michael Mitton*, A Heart to Listen, *2010*

While we were learning not to speak too soon in regard to Scotty, we were also learning not to provide answers too quickly with his housemate, Paul.

Paul had dropped out of school at a young age but was actually very bright. He had the gift of the gab and, as he would say, could 'turn a fiver into a tenner'.

He was also illiterate. We saw this challenge and came up with a solution: literacy lessons. We asked him, probably in a way he couldn't refuse, whether he wanted such lessons and then arranged them for him. He didn't turn up. We did the same thing again and had the same results. Eventually, we gave up, sighing, 'Pah! We go to all this trouble for people, and this is how they repay us.' The trouble was, of course, we hadn't listened. We had come with a hero mentality, looking to solve what we thought was a problem. Paul had managed his whole life – now into his forties – without reading. What he cared more about was coming off methadone. He kept saying that in order to come off it, he needed to do a bike ride round Britain. We thought this was both mad and dangerous.

However, he kept going on about it, so eventually I had a meeting with him and Graham to talk about the idea. Once again, he explained his plan, which still seemed mad and dangerous. Graham and I were exchanging looks of cynicism, but then, in what felt like a wave of the Holy Spirit, Graham declared, 'Well, if the Lord is in this, who can be against it? Let's do this thing.'

We all agreed, and over the next few months we clucked around Paul as he got his bike and a carrier together. We helped him with other preparations, including teaching him how to read a map ('Keep the coast to your left when you're going west'). The process of focusing on all this gave Paul the hope and purpose to get through drug withdrawal, 'cold turkey' style.[1] Graham drove him to Dover, and off he went. We heard he got to Brighton, and then Cornwall, within a few weeks. He was used to camping out, so being in a tent on the south coast was a joy to him.

I learned a lot through this experience. People know what their needs are better than we do. Trusting them, listening to them, building on their strengths (in this case, a love of biking), rather than trying to fix their perceived weaknesses, is a more sustainable approach to 'empowering' them. It also means recognizing the inner hero or mother hen in oneself and repressing it.

Paul did manage to come off methadone completely by doing his cycle ride. Unfortunately, he slipped back into bad habits a wee while after his return. Too well known to the dealers and unable to shake off his reputation, he reverted to some of his old ways. However, he eventually left for Brighton, and the last we heard was that he was doing well there.

While we were busy with Paul, we met a man called Sam who had a six-year relationship with heroin and had been living in a hostel in Cambridge for over five years. Sam did not know where his parents lived; they had moved and deliberately not told him their new address, a heart-wrenching decision they had had to make to protect their goods and money from being stolen. That is what heroin does: it turns sons against their mothers, tearing into the heart of families.

I knew Sam was struggling with his mental health, and I really wasn't sure whether I could work with him. Was he too 'high need'?

Did I need more training? However, I also knew he was trying to change and really wanted a place of his own where he could reboot his life, as his hostel contained memories and associations he could do without. I could see that he had a good heart and was desperate to move in, so we decided we would take him on.

In those early days, despite my fears, Sam proved a joy to work with. We could see the immediate impact that his new living arrangement had on him. His health, sleep and diet all improved. In the space of a few days, he felt he had a home that he could be proud of, and he invited his parents to visit. Within a week they were at the house and he was preparing a barbecue for them.

As Christmas came – a time of great challenge for many – Sam's change of circumstances showed in special ways.

'Ed,' he said to me excitedly, 'look at all my Christmas cards! I have twelve cards! I haven't had a single card for years.'

It is often the small acts of kindness that make a difference. Not only did he have cards; he also had company, spending the whole of Christmas Day in the home of a church family.

Slowly, Sam's relationship with his parents improved. They felt they could give him their address; then they allowed him to visit and then to stay overnight. The following Christmas, he celebrated with his relatives in the family home for the first time in eight years. Finally, the next year, his parents wrote him back into their will.

If that is not an endorsement of the change Sam had made, then little else would be.

Earning the trust and feeling the love of immediate family is fundamental to our sense of wholeness. When I travel abroad, I instantly miss my wife and children, from the moment I get on a plane to the second I get back. No matter how long I am away for, there is an ache and hole in my heart every moment they are not there. So too with many of our tenants: they feel the detachment of having lost contact and relationship with their nearest and dearest. We often find that within days or weeks of coming into our homes, they get back in touch with their children, their parents or their siblings. We see their wholeness being restored through those rekindled relationships.

Sam is still a friend of ours at Hope into Action. He has now moved back to Cambridge to be nearer his family. His mental health is still a battle, he remains on methadone – albeit a much smaller dosage – and he still struggles with life. The difference is that now he has people he can call up when he is in a difficult spot: his mother, his father, his sisters, and two close friends from church. It is now to them he turns first when a girlfriend has dumped him, his benefits have been cut or he has fallen out with his neighbour. His social capital – his relational richness – is now enhanced and, as a consequence, so too is his resilience to the shocks of life.

After Sam had moved into our home, we had a vacancy for a housemate for him, and we thought about offering a room to a man called Rob, who was struggling with addiction. However, we felt uncertain about working with Rob and unsure of how he would get on. He was a high-calibre man, with an ability to be both wise and articulate, but we had to think carefully about whether we should take him in. He had been on the streets on and off for the best part of 20 years. In that time, he had done at least two stints in rehabilitation, but, with nowhere to go and no one to go to, he had been back on heroin within days of leaving.

Rob had a gruff-looking street face, and his arms were marked with tattoos. Yet in my initial meeting with him, he spent the best part of the first 20 minutes in tears as he recounted his experiences of being a soldier in Northern Ireland and unpacked how post-traumatic stress disorder (PTSD) had left him still suffering nightmares 20 years on. After talking with him, we arranged for him to meet those we were working with at the church. He turned up to the meeting drunk, and at that point we really were not sure how wise it would be to proceed.

In the end, after a further few weeks of meeting up with him, we decided we would go for it. A few months later he decided that the last day of the year would be the last day he took any heroin substitutes. Although he had detoxed from heroin in rehabilitation before, this time he came off 'in community'. That first week of January was really tough and he was very unwell, but once he was through, he had made it. He still faced some pretty major battles: benefits were cut, old associates found him, he got arrested for a crime he hadn't committed, poor health assailed him, and more. It was as if the devil were prowling round him, attacking him, seeking to devour his flesh.[2]

Six years on, Rob is still clean from heroin. His life has been far from easy, but he now seems to have found his way. I count him as a dear friend. He has done numerous public talks with me, and we have spent hours together on the road attending events. I always find he steals the show. He has an amazing ability to hold people's attention. He doesn't shout; he speaks slowly and eloquently, and he is prepared to tell his story and make himself vulnerable. When he talks about what helped him come through, he mentions the support from the church during that time and, in particular, a men's group he belonged to. He also talks of the power of acts of kindness, such as when someone paid off a £300 debt for him. He remains clean to this day and is now able to help others with addictions.

Along the path of all these relationships, we have learned a few lessons. We try hard not to judge, and we pray for wisdom to know when and how to speak the truth. We have learned to listen, rather than dive in with our own solutions.

Unconditional, non-judgmental listening is key. As I read through the Scriptures, I see that Jesus was not just a great preacher and healer, but also a fabulous listener. (We just don't hear many preachers preaching about Jesus listening.) Time and again, we see him starting conversations with a question. Someone once told me that Jesus was asked 80 questions (precious few he seemed to answer), but that he himself asked 300. Therefore, to be like Christ is to ask four times as many questions as we are asked. It is to be constantly listening. Jesus seems to understand people and situations so well, as we can tell from the repeated comments in the Gospels that he acted after having 'heard' or having 'seen' something. It is from a place of really hearing people that we are able to build relationships, trust, confidence and hope for change. Listening is also the impetus to action.

Healing will take a lifetime for many of the men and women who have been through an addiction, because 'healing' is so much more than the removal of physical craving. That is hard enough, but the drug use has often been there to block and suppress pain that resides underneath, which then resurfaces as the addiction is dealt with. Healing is physical, psychological and relational.

Increasingly, scientific studies are coming to the conclusion (and the charity sector is increasingly recognizing) that heroin addiction is actually a 'disease of unconnectedness', meaning that it replaces our deep human need to be connected and loved. One of the arguments that is often given to support this involves a study on rats. I am slightly wary of comparing humans to rats, but the study makes an interesting observation. In the experiment, rats were given the choice of two water bottles, one with clean water and one laced with heroin. When the experiment was carried out with rats living alone in separate cages, they all became addicted to heroin (only ever drinking from the heroin bottle) and displayed unusual and aggressive behaviour, before dying prematurely. When the experiment was conducted on rats living in 'rat heaven' – a large cage with loads of exercise wheels and other rats to interact and play with – none of the rats became addicted.

The researchers concluded that those in addiction need 'connectedness', or 'social capital' as some studies call it. We call it 'love'. If one takes this theory forward and accepts that connectedness, or love, is a vital part of recovery, it is significant that the response of our society to addiction often involves social isolation. It is not uncommon to find addicts criminalized, and then further ostracized and shamed by being locked away in cells.

The above is a synopsis of a much larger debate, and of course there are many more layers of complexity to it. However, I would be comfortable arguing – and indeed I strongly believe – that there is significant truth in the theory that addiction is, in part at least, a disease of unconnectedness. For this reason, we feel confident about the approach of our model, which places relationships at its heart, for helping those who are suffering with addictions or are coming out of rehabilitation.

23

Manna from heaven

God is able to bless you abundantly, so that in all things at
all times, having all that you need, you will abound in every
good work.

–2 Corinthians 9.8

During the initial phase of opening homes, my godmother
brought some of her friends to a talk I gave in Cambridge. After
the meeting one of her friends said to me, 'We so need this in
Norwich. When do you think you'll be able to set something up
there?'

'I think we're about two years away,' was my considered reply,
given that our resources were stretched to full capacity.

'Two years!' she exclaimed. 'We can't wait that long. I'll try to get
you to speak in the next two months.'

And so she did. Evidently, my opinions and our readiness did
not matter. Two months later, there I was in Norwich giving a talk.

The wheels in Norwich were now turning and much was to
follow. That initial conversation with my godmother's tenacious
friend was to give birth to one of the most profound moments in all
my work at Hope into Action.

While I was still feeling I could not manage one more thing, I
received a call from a vicar in Nottingham called Dave Hammond.
He explained that he was based in The Meadows, the second
poorest estate in Nottingham, and that he would like to set up a
homeless house in the area.

As I was feeling tired and stressed at the time, I explained that
my wife was about to give birth to our third child (a neat bit of 'my

life is busier than yours' one-upmanship) and asked if he would mind calling me back in one month.

'Sure thing,' came the sprightly reply. 'I fully understand. My wife is also pregnant with our third child. [Touché.] Will do.'

I had had plenty of such conversations before, so as I put down the phone I wasn't sure if I would ever hear from him again. However, as I was to discover, Dave was not a man to be deterred.

Early in 2012, Rach went into labour. It was clearly God's timing as it coincided with both the Australian Open tennis championship and England playing cricket in Pakistan. So it meant that between contractions, as well as giving Rach my undivided attention, I was able to follow the progress of Roger Federer and the English fast bowlers. At one stage I thought Rach was going to produce a delivery that Jimmy Anderson would be proud of. In the end, it was far more heroic than that. Jos was eventually born by caesarean section, blond and strong. (It's good we have a relationship of trust, as I am dark-haired and lanky.) I wondered again at how such an innocent, non-communicative being could hold such power over a man's heart. I soon discovered that parenting two girls had not fully prepared me for a son. As I changed his first nappy, my mind was suddenly awash with the thought: what a big bladder he must have! And then: do I try to dry my jeans or should I change them?

Shortly after the birth, Rach declared, 'I'm never going through that again' (referring to childbirth, not, thankfully, the act that got her into that situation). So I soon found myself lying on my back with an elderly Far Eastern nurse saying to me, 'Okay, Mista Woka, pease pow dow your pants.' With the lady now staring at my indignity, the doctor made the snip.

Just before Jos was born, we began to realize we needed a finance administrator at Hope into Action. I discussed this with Gavin Bateman and he wisely suggested, and I agreed, that maybe we should pray about it because, you never know, God might provide a volunteer. Wise as this advice from Gavin was, I can't remember ever actually praying about it. (Most spare time in this phase of my life was spent dropping off to sleep.) I assume that Gavin did, however, because shortly after Jos's birth, a woman called Liz Hallam got in touch. Although we had been in the same church for a while, we had never properly met. We arranged a 'getting to know each other' coffee, over which she informed me that she had a background in . . . finance administration. It took all my management acumen to suggest we might have a role that fitted her skills. She arrived to find our finances in no end of a mess (please don't tell our donors) and lovingly whipped us into shape. In the end, she humbly gave us five years of her time two days a week, never asking for anything, barely claiming expenses, but always doing a brilliant job. I am convinced people like Liz will be right at the front of the queue for heaven's riches!

And then Dave Hammond, the vicar from Nottingham, called back.

By now I was no less tired and no less stressed than I was the previous month when I had tried to fob him off. I attempted again to cold-shoulder him: 'Well, to take on this project, you really need to make sure the church is committed to it.'

'No problem. I'm the leader.'

'Okay. Well, you will need to have a small group of committed volunteers.'

'No problem; I can arrange that. Anything else?'

Trying to shake him off: 'Well, you really need at least thirty to forty thousand pounds of capital to get a house sorted.'

'Ah, I'm not sure how we could do that. We're only a small church, and most members of our congregation come from our local estate. I'm not sure we can do anything. It will need a miracle.'

'Oh, well,' I said, trying to hide my relief, 'that's a shame. Do give me a call back if you find the money.' I ended the conversation with a cheery 'God bless', put the phone down and cracked on with my next task. Once again, I did not expect the conversation to go any further.

Twenty minutes later the phone rang.

'Hi, Ed, it's Dave.'

'Hi, Dave, how are you?' I replied, suppressing my irritation.

'You'll never believe this, but I've just found thirty thousand pounds!'

'*What?!*'

He explained that after I had told him he would need £30,000 he put the phone down, prayed, walked out of his study into the church office, and the first thing a parishioner said was: 'Dave, we completely forgot about a repayment we were due, and it's just come through. We'll get it any day. It should be thirty to forty thousand pounds. We'd like it to be used for the Lord somehow. Do you have any ideas what we might do with it?'

And that is how we got our first house in Nottingham.

We have now opened our seventh home in Nottingham. We have housed many people, seen former addicts give up their addictions, provided a home for many refugees, had former prostitutes completely come off drugs and come to faith, and much more. We had one tenant who had been in prison over 40 times before, and it was a joy to see that cycle broken as he stayed out of jail and came off the prolific offender list for the first time in 20 years. As I write this, I have just come back from speaking at a partner church in Nottingham. I was greeted warmly by two former sex workers who have moved on from our house and are doing well. It all stemmed from that phone call and the pestering, faith-filled nature of a wonderful man, now my friend, called Dave Hammond.

The amazing details of how each of our houses has come into being are etched in my memory. In every case it has felt as though manna has dropped from heaven. Behind each home we have opened is a wonderful story of grace, generosity, 'coincidence' and church engagement. At times now, as I match investors with churches, it feels as though I am just shuffling miracles around the country into our 25-plus cities. And it still excites me. It is amazing to see the vision becoming a reality: people sharing their wealth with the poor, and the Church giving the homeless a home.

24

'I suggest they pray outside – at 3 a.m.'

[Abraham's] faith and his actions were working together, and his faith was made complete by what he did.

–James 2.22

While our work in Nottingham had been getting going, we had won a government social enterprise grant of £90,000 to buy a house. The pressure to find a property was intense, as we had to complete the purchase within six months. I desperately wanted to be able to use the grant rather than lose it.

I therefore approached a church leader to see if his church wanted to partner with us. After a few conversations, he took the idea to his leadership team. It was a dark, wintery afternoon when I picked up his email. He informed me that the leaders had said they would need to 'pray about it and seek God's will for at least another month'.

This was a blow; time was not on our side. I looked out of the window and studied the drizzling rain as it hit the pane of glass. I reread the email and pondered my response as I tracked a droplet zigzagging its way south.

Then out it came:

Thank you very much for your email. As your leadership team are praying about this for the next month, might I suggest they commit to doing their praying between 3.00 and 4.00 in the morning. Every morning. Please could you ask them to do their praying outside, while walking around the city centre? And perhaps they can use this prayer: 'Lord, we have been offered a house to house the homeless. I know you care for the poor – it's written on every page of the Bible. Please reveal your will.' And once they have prayed that prayer, perhaps you might ask them, as they walk past someone sleeping in a bag, to consider this scripture which I will happily cut out for each of them: 'What good is it, my brothers or sisters, if someone claims to have faith but has no deeds? . . . Suppose a brother or sister is without clothes and daily food. If one of you says to them, "Go in peace; keep warm and well fed," but does nothing about his physical needs, what good is it? In the same way, faith by itself, if it is not accompanied by action, is dead.'[1]

Lots of love,
Ed

Send.

As I cycled home in the rain, I began to consider the wisdom of such a response.

Needless to say, the church did not partner with us, and my relationship with that church leader was never quite the same again.

I have realized over the years that my drive and passion come from two places within me. One is a genuine compassion for my fellow human beings; the other is anger at church indifference. The second may sound less 'holy', but I have come to wonder whether it is no less reflective of the heart of God. Love for the poor must generate passion to address indifference towards suffering.

However, managing that passion has proven more difficult than managing compassion, as I demonstrated with my email.

I have tried to learn that charm works better than aggression, and patience better than sarcasm. Over the following years I have managed (mostly) to keep my fat gob shut. I now also have far more empathy for church leaders, who have an impossible job description. I recognize that, while I can focus on one area of ministry, they have to manage every current and potential area of ministry. However, while I'm not proud of it, that email at least gives an insight into where much of my drive comes from. It is what gets me up in the morning and pushes me so hard.

I went, instead, to the local branch of the Salvation Army, where I received a keener and more timely response. The leader, Adrian Maddern, an inspiring man who had spent many years working with people on the street, was quick to show his support. 'It's what we should be doing,' he responded enthusiastically. I found my reaction to his enthusiasm came in more diplomatic tones than I'd managed to use in my email.

Adrian's denomination has a long tradition of working with the community at the heart of some of the most challenging areas of Peterborough. However, near his branch there were very few houses going for £90,000, even fewer with sellers able to move quickly. Eventually, we found a suitable property within a mile of the church. We couldn't get the seller down below £94,000, but with time ticking rapidly on, we had to agree on terms. We literally had no idea where the balance would come from. About two weeks later, an elderly gentleman randomly phoned up and said he had about £5,000 coming to fruition in his stewardship account. Could we please explain how our housing model stacked up and let him know whether we could do with the money to go towards a house?

This was an amazing answer to prayer. At this stage no single individual had ever given us anywhere near that sum of money. (We had had larger investments, but never such a large donation.)

The legal shenanigans for this house were the most difficult we have dealt with, but somehow, with a highly harangued solicitor, we completed the purchase on 31 March, the last day possible. The next challenge was where we would get the money to refurbish the property. We received a grant from the council that covered

£1,000, but how would we find the remaining £8,000 that was needed?

The phone rang again. It was the elderly gentleman: 'I've looked again at the account and have another eight thousand pounds in it. My wife and I are getting old and would like to get rid of the money as fast as we can. Any ideas?'

Er, well, yes, actually . . .

Meanwhile, three volunteers from the church, Ken, Karen and Judith, had come forward to be part of the 'Friendship and Support Group'. They proved to be a great team and were a joy to work with: down to earth, wise and spiritual.

A prison resettlement officer referred a man called Brian to us for consideration as a potential tenant. He had a long history of offences, but we did some digging and felt he was worth visiting. The son of a pastor, he was a good-looking, stocky lad who played drums in the prison chapel and had been a talented footballer in his youth. His big doe-like brown eyes and charming, deep-toned voice exuded just enough vulnerability to help us all fall in love with him. When the time came for his release, Karen and Ken were there to meet him at the gate. They took him to the local supermarket to buy his favourite foods and then brought him back to the house.

After offloading the shopping and looking round the garden and lounge with Ken, Brian went upstairs to see his bedroom. There he found Karen on her knees making his bed.

When I saw Brian the next day, all he could say was: 'I can't believe she was making my bed. Ed, she was making my bed!'

'I know,' came my reply, 'because you've already told me five times!'

We played everything by the book with Brian. He was a genuinely lovable guy. He was also well connected with plenty of the locals (many of whom he had known in prison) as Karen and Ken had discovered on that first trip round the supermarket, when he seemed to know every second person in the store.

Within three months the relationship was heading south. Brian never had any money, but somehow he had acquired a car. Before we knew it, he had been recalled to prison.

I had the task of clearing out his room, and it was a depressing insight into a poorly managed life, one with so much potential failing to be realized: debt letters, documentation of failed meetings with the council, a photo of his estranged child, a few stray Bible verses, the odd letter from a family member, cigarette papers, a suitcase still filled with unpacked clothes, a strange empty bottle with a pipe sticking out of it, a picture of him playing football as a youth, more cigarette papers and tobacco . . .

We were gutted. I was gutted. We had done everything the experts said should be done.

I happened to be at the prison a couple of weeks later and sought Brian out. After he had petitioned me to do something about the car, we had a more real and honest conversation than we had ever had while he was free.

This all happened just before my summer holiday. Rach and I took our three kids in a small caravan to the Gower peninsula in Wales and had a great time in the wettest August for ten years. I took the opportunity to read through all the Gospels, searching for clues about how Jesus operated and what we were missing.

I noticed that every single miracle, bar two, occurred when people came to Jesus. I looked at blind Bartimaeus.[2] He screamed out to Jesus. Everyone told him to shut up, but he kept screaming. Then Jesus stopped. I thought about how much the bleeding woman wanted the miracle, and about how Jesus tested the Canaanite mother.[3]

For miracles to happen in one of our houses, I concluded, the prospective tenants have to really want the house. The tenants have to want the house more than we want them in it. We have to make the assessment process a test of this desire.

We have tried to follow that principle ever since.

A few weeks after coming back from my holiday, I met an ex-tenant called Ewan wandering around near the station.

'How are you, Ewan?' I asked in a sprightly tone.

'Not good,' came the glum reply. 'I'm at my lowest point.'

'Oh dear.'

'I've never been so depressed; I'm surrounded by scumbags, and I can't stop drinking. I'm on about twenty-six cans a day. For the first time in my life, I've just prayed for help – and now I've met you. Can you help?'

Remembering the lessons from my holiday, I told him he would have to come to see me in the office the next day.

He turned up. I told him about a church leader, Maggie, in nearby Gunthorpe. 'Go and visit her and do two weeks volunteering at her food bank,' I said. 'She'll let me know how you're getting on.'

'What? Ed, that's harsh! I didn't have to do that last time.'

'No,' I replied, 'and last time you didn't engage with us very well. I need to see you want this. We will only take you on if you're serious about dealing with your drinking.'

Ewan passed the test. He clearly wanted to change. We gave him a home. He slowly reduced his drinking. At the same time, the church helped him work out a way to clear his debts through its Christians Against Poverty (CAP) debt centre. After a year or so, he had reduced his alcohol intake enough to go into detox. Maggie took him to the centre, visited from time to time and picked him up when he was due to be discharged. A few months later he had moved on, was debt free, had remained drink free and had got a job. There was healing and there was holistic change. The last time I saw him, he was married and working full time in the prison.

As I write this draft today, I've 'liked' Ewan's social media post celebrating his third year sober. I remembered those words from Isaiah about breaking '*every* yoke',[4] and allowed myself a moment to rejoice at how well this young man had done and what a privilege it had been to journey alongside him.

25

'God is there for you in the darkest pit'

Nothing can ever separate us from God's love.

–Romans 8.38 NLT

The wheels had been continuing to turn in Norwich, thanks to my godmother's dynamic friend. Around the time I was reconnecting with Ewan, we opened a house there, run in partnership with Norwich Central Baptist Church, to support women coming out of a drugs rehabilitation centre.

We did some great work with the ladies in that home. I used to think that once someone got clean through rehab, that was the end of the matter. Job done. The reality is very far from that; many go back to using drugs afterwards. I had a good insight into this through my colleague Tom Ward, who spent ten years working in a rehab and watching the good work unravel at the point of transition into the community. Tom saw how the dealers would be at the door waiting, and decided to set up a Hope into Action house in his home town of Reading to deal with this flaw in the system. I remember him telling me, 'Those dealers are brilliant at marketing – they greet former drug users as they come out of prison, they meet them as they leave the rehab and they even find them at the Narcotics Anonymous groups. We Christians have to outmanoeuvre them!'

I vividly remember meeting one of our early tenants, Jane. I had just preached a sermon at Norwich Central Baptist Church on how Jesus was willing to risk his life to save the adulterous woman who was being abused by multiple men.[1] Jane was pretty and slim, and looked young, with short dark hair cut in a bob around her pale face. Her eyes revealed both a sharp intelligence and a vulnerability that suggested something of her 'life challenges'. After chatting to her at the end of the service, I ended by giving her an awkward side-on Christian hug (I'm English, after all).

A few weeks later I was back with our empowerment worker, Kate, having to evict Jane. That was a pretty horrible experience. She stared back as I delivered the news, accepting her fate with a lamb-like expression, sweet and innocent-looking (though, as she won't mind me saying, looks can of course be deceiving).

Kate was amazing and, despite having three kids and a caseload with us, kept in constant contact with Jane even though she was no longer a tenant.

Some time later, Jane wrote about her experience with us:

NFA – No Fixed Abode – that was how I lived my whole adult life. I spent my late teenage years bouncing around foster homes, hostels and detox centres, until I finally resigned myself to the streets. Eventually, I found myself in a rehab and, by the skin of my teeth, I made it through six months there. As I walked out of the doors of the rehab, someone finally decided to take a chance on me. I was a recipe for relapse, accidental death or suicide, and yet they took a chance. Hope into Action housed me and gave me a roof over my head. They gave me a fixed address for the first time since I was a girl.

Less than a month later, I sat opposite my empowerment worker in a tiny café and took a deep breath before getting honest and telling her that I had, yet again, breached the terms of my agreement. She told me that she would have to evict me – something I was more than used to. As I walked out of that café to try to find somewhere I could sleep that night, I was certain it was the end of my experience with Hope into

Action, and that after I moved my things out I'd never see my empowerment worker again.

I was wrong. In reality, it was the beginning of my relationship with Hope into Action, and what happened over the following two years showed me what Hope into Action is all about. I spent the next two years back in my old life, using heavy drugs, prostituting myself and bouncing around hostels. I overdosed several times. Everyone had given up on me again, and any hope I once had was crushed. My empowerment worker would text me regularly, would meet me for a coffee or give me a hug when she bumped into me in the city. In the midst of my mess, chaos and despair, she held on to hope and faith for me. When I couldn't see past my next bag of heroin, she saw a bright future for me and regularly told me about it. She loved me relentlessly, never gave up hope and prayed persistently. When God felt so far away, so judgmental, so punishing, she was 'hope with skin on' to me. She loved me in a way I couldn't feel from an invisible God. It took two long years until she finally received a text from me: 'I can't do this any more, I need to get clean, and I need something different, I think I need God.'

A year later, I stood at the front of the annual Hope into Action conference sharing some of my story. The rest of the day was spent interacting with the various people who had attended, hearing their hearts and their stories. As the conference came to an end, I looked around the room and felt overwhelmed with love and gratitude. I finally understood that the love my empowerment worker had shown me wasn't just what *she* was about; it was what Hope into Action was about. An organization and churches made up of people who genuinely love and care for people like me, for the people whom society generally rejects. A group of people who want to walk alongside some of the messiest people and love them in any way they can. People who will hold on to hope and faith for as long as is necessary, not just when it's easy or convenient but also when it would be so easy to give up: when it's hard and dark.

To me, Hope into Action is a charity that takes chances on the people no one else will; an organization that, even when they have to make tough choices, never gives up; a network of staff and churches who want to walk alongside people through the swampy mess and not simply welcome them on the banks of acceptability; a group of people who try to personify the heart of God, who become 'Jesus with skin on' to those who can't find or trust the invisible God. I am privileged, proud and forever grateful to be connected to such a group of people, and so thankful that they took a chance on me and always held on to hope, even when I could not.

Jane's participation at our conference was a profound moment for me. I felt a real sense of joy to be able to interview her (at her request) that day, and her words captured everything I hoped for when I set up Hope into Action. She spoke powerfully and eloquently in front of 250 people from around England. I still remember how encouraged I was to hear her say, 'Hope into Action helped save my life, not only by housing me when I needed it, but also by giving me continued support after I left. They have loved me at my worst, fought for me continually and encouraged me endlessly.'

I then asked her about the messages she had received from churches over the years, and she replied, 'Churches and Christians sometimes share a message that if you get "clean" then you will get God's love, when the message you should be sending is that God is there for you even when you're in the darkest pit.'

It was one of those 'pin drop' and 'light bulb' moments. A pin drop moment because it was clear that the whole audience was absolutely absorbed by everything Jane was saying: in the silence you could literally have heard a pin drop. A light bulb moment because she somehow made us all see that we had been getting it wrong.

In the way God so often does, he used the humble to lovingly teach the proud. In that room were academics, theologians, church leaders and no end of do-gooders like myself. Yet despite all our years of church attendance and Bible reading, God used a recovering addict with a history of prostitution to highlight to us our own inner harshness and our rule-driven rather than grace-driven approach. He did it in such a gentle and unobtrusive way that no one could take offence or argue with it.

We put on loads of great speakers and events after that point, but in the feedback at the end, almost everyone mentioned that moment as the highlight of the day.

At the conference, Jane collected an award for staying off drugs. In contrast to so many messages she had received in her time, she was now being congratulated by the General Director of the Evangelical Alliance for her remarkable achievements.

26

Iain Duncan Smith

Speak up for those who cannot speak for themselves, for the rights of all who are destitute.

–Proverbs 31.8

Around the time we were opening the Norwich house, I was sitting at home in the evening fumbling around on Twitter. I am not really an avid user of Twitter, but I had been told that our local Member of Parliament, Stewart Jackson, had put out an important tweet: Iain Duncan Smith, then Secretary of State for Work and Pensions, was coming to Peterborough and wanted to see a local charity at work. After a fair bit of confusion, I managed to find the relevant tweet and reply, asking him to consider Hope into Action.

Amazingly, we were chosen!

While I was waiting to hear if Iain Duncan Smith might visit us, I was really hoping he would. However, as soon as I heard he was coming, I began to regret it and wondered what we would do with him and how we would handle his visit.

We decided to take him to the house that had been owned by James Adams, who had died in the 7/7 bombing, and that had been bought by the former police officer Steve to house former prisoners.

On the day of Iain Duncan Smith's arrival, we were waiting to meet him at Bretton Baptist Church so that we could escort him to the house. I was with Steve and David, my minister, and we were accompanied by a good-sized media contingent.

Iain Duncan Smith's car drove up and he appeared, carrying himself with military comportment, and greeted me with a good shake of the hand: warm but professional. The journalists interviewed him first and then we briefed him, discussing our concerns regarding the benefits system, in particular as it related to those leaving prison.

After the discussions, we drove over to the house and I introduced him to the tenants, one of whom was also called Iain. As we stood in the kitchen, the tenants did a good job of grilling the cabinet minister and conveying their concerns.

I don't agree with all of Iain Duncan Smith's views – far from it – but I did get the impression that he listened, he was on top of his brief, and he actually cared and wanted the system to work.

It was a special moment to see our house being used not only for hope and restoration, but also to entertain and advocate to one of the most powerful individuals in the UK.

While meeting Iain Duncan Smith was a memorable occasion, our next tenant in the house was to make a much greater impact on me.

27

Krish

The greatest disease in the West today is not TB or leprosy; it is being unwanted, unloved and uncared for. We can cure physical diseases with medicine, but the only cure for loneliness, despair and hopelessness is love.

–Mother Teresa

The winter of 2012/13 was brutal – the worst in 20 years in the UK – with temperatures plummeting to below -5 °C (23 °F), alongside high rainfall. The February chill with its icy winds seemed to bite through the thickest woollies, and the March weather was the coldest since 1962. I can still remember, in the midst of the gruelling conditions, reflecting on how hard it must be to be homeless.

I won't forget meeting Krish during that time, nor the things he taught me. He was different from many we knew: his life was in the shadows, but it had once been in the limelight. He also scared me. He scared me because I could see the reflection of my upbringing, my friends and myself in him. Like me, he had been to a good school. He had done well, got married, had three children, and built a successful career and business.

We met him in the February of that freezing winter. He had been walking the streets of Cambridge for six weeks. He found it too cold to sleep during the night, so would just huddle in wind-protected nooks and crannies. In the early morning he would trek five miles to a service station near the A14 to take a shower. Then he would walk back to the library and spend his time reading (to keep his mind distracted) and dozing, before another dark, icy night beset him.

Krish came from a culture that had very strong community and kinship bonds. His own family was both wealthy and influential. As a young man, Krish had been a successful sportsman. He went on to run a sizeable antiques business. He owned a large home and a smart car. However, he then went bankrupt, and, at the same time, his family discovered he had been having an affair. They would have nothing further to do with him.

Those once-powerful bonds of support, with which he had been nurtured and raised, were now gone. Krish discovered the inverted force of their power in rejection.

The shock hit him hard. Being on the streets was a trauma. How had it come to this? How had he ended up here? On top of all that, he was now experiencing racial abuse and even violence. He found himself completely alone and ill-equipped.

Processing all that would take time.

We met Krish, helped him and gave him a home in Steve's house. Taking him there was quite a contrast to the last time I had brought someone to the property six months earlier, when Iain Duncan Smith had visited.

After a while Krish was ready to move on, and we found him a flat to rent and provided the deposit to secure it. I happened to be there on the day he moved, and helped him carry his belongings up to his apartment on the third floor. Despite the wealth of his family, he remained penniless; no one had given him work and he was still living off benefits. In addition, his blood pressure was dangerously high.

As we lugged the furniture up the stairs, he told me about his family. I could sense his pain as he shared with me how his mother had cut him off, had suffered two strokes and now was dying. He worried they would never meet again, let alone make peace. His brother was the managing director of a well-known company. Long before the alienation, he had honoured Krish by naming his daughter with the feminine version of Krish's name. Now, however, when she got married, he had not even invited Krish to her wedding. The last Krish had heard of his own 12-year-old son was that he had got into a football academy with a Premier League club. However, he had been blocked from being able to watch his son play by his former wife.

Once, Krish had brought pride to the family name; now it was shame and dishonour. There was no forgiveness, no wedding attendance, no watching his son, no contact with his daughters, no loving reassurance from his mother.

I often hear the charge against Christianity that it has caused a lot of wars. I can see the point (although I would usually try to add, 'Judge a spade by how it's designed, not by how it's used' – you wouldn't blame the designer if someone used it to hit someone else). However, there is another side to the story which often doesn't get mentioned: Jesus says he came to save us from our sins.[1] But how exactly does that play out here on earth, and how does that relate to a family like Krish's?

If I am wronged, I instinctively feel angry, bitter and upset, alongside a range of other emotions – just as, I imagine, Krish's wife must have felt. I don't instinctively feel the desire to forgive, nor do I find it easy to do so. I like the way Archbishop Desmond Tutu puts it: anyone who thinks forgiveness is for the weak has clearly never tried it.

Yet most people in the West, Christian or otherwise, teach their children to forgive and to say sorry.

If I had an affair, the natural order of reactions would mean I would be ostracized. If, instead, my wife, my brother and my mother were to forgive me, allowing me love and access to my family, then I would be saved from the consequences of my sins. This concept of forgiveness is something Jesus and his followers have done much to spread. Jesus promoted the radical notion that we should forgive those who persecute us, and love our enemies. He then embodied those noble virtues in his death, healing a soldier who had come to arrest him, and praying 'Father, forgive them' as he hung on the cross.[2] His disciples then risked their lives to propagate the message of forgiveness and love even further,[3] and it has been spread by countless others over the centuries since. If Krish's family were to embrace forgiveness, he would be freed from much of his emotional torture or, to put it in Christian language, the consequence of his sins.

Many others have experienced such freedom through the pardoning of sins larger and smaller than Krish's. Jesus' promotion of forgiveness has brought psychological and emotional healing – as any objective, reasonable mind must accept – to millions upon millions of people. Spreading a message of forgiveness (the good news of Jesus) is an undeniably noble and honourable cause, one the disciples were prepared to die for, and one I am at least prepared to commit my life to. I had never seen the Christian message in such terms until I met Krish.

I am still in touch with Krish. His blood pressure remains high and he has suffered a stroke. He is rebuilding a relationship with his parents – though, sadly, not yet with his children – and has now remarried. We sometimes talk about forgiveness. I'm not sure how deep it goes. He does occasionally light a candle in a Cambridge chapel, and every now and then stays on for a service. Staring at his experience of unforgiveness helped me appreciate the gospel's power so much more. May he, and others in his situation, find forgiveness here on earth as it is in heaven!

Krish also taught me something of mutuality – a sense that my humanity is made more complete in another's humanity.

I think I started Hope into Action with a kind of rescuer mentality. I grew up wanting to be a firefighter and then spent nine years in Africa flying into hotspots. Over time, I have come to see how this approach can be unhelpful. We are not coming along like a knight in shining armour to a damsel in distress (though there are times I think we do a bit of that – sometimes appropriately, but usually not). Our outlook is rather that, while many people have indeed experienced love through us (and many have responded to that love in positive ways), we also believe, and observe, that through these encounters we ourselves find God. Our experience reveals that meaning in life can actually be found in the shadows and in relating to those whom others rush past while trying to get ahead. When we create time to listen to those in the margins of society, life can be put into perspective, and, in a very real way, God speaks to us.

Not a year goes by that I don't read a book about people who have been on the streets, on drugs, in prison or abused, but who then come to know God and see their lives turned around. I read these accounts to understand more deeply the issues and lives of our tenants and also to encourage my faith. We now have a lot of such stories ourselves. At least once a month we share one internally and take time to stop, pray and celebrate. So many of our tenants' stories deserve a book all to themselves, and I would love to write them all. When you consider the background of these men and women, you realize their strength and courage is amazing.

You may have encountered such stories at Christian festivals, where one or two people get up and share for a couple of minutes about how they were once in a mess and now their life is in order. I find these testimonies to be a tremendous encouragement. Stories strengthen faith, and at Hope into Action we can certainly tell of many people kicking habits, re-engaging with family, finding faith, converting, and responding to altar calls. We rejoice with all of these.

However, we've also learned that sustainable success does not just happen overnight. It doesn't happen in a 'moment'. Spiritual moments happen, but for the fledgling faith not to 'quickly fall away', 'wither' or 'choke',[4] – for the faith to be sustainable – it should be supported by people willing and committed to journey with the new believer, and be in it for the long haul.

Indeed, in virtually every one of our best testimonies, and the testimonies I have read, there are three key ingredients:

1 *A safe home.* The person has to have a home. It is extraordinarily hard to sort one's life out when one is on the streets, fighting for survival.
2 *Grace.* After a home, the person needs grace. Almost always there is someone in the story who has journeyed with him or her, and almost always that individual has had to show grace because the road to recovery has not been a straight one. (Show me a recovering addict who claims to have never relapsed, and I will show you a liar.)
3 *Time.* Lasting change takes time. Probably not months; more likely years. It almost never happens overnight.

A home, a companion and patience – sometimes years of patience. This is what we try to bring. Many academic papers and studies have found something similar. While the researchers use different language and 'evidence', essentially recovery boils down to those three elements.

'Good grief,' I hear you sigh. 'Is this type of outreach really for me, then?' To which we thunder back 'Yes!' Being with those who have spent some of their life 'in the shadows' should be part of what Christians are all about. It should be seen as essential Christian living, taught in Sunday school and youth groups just after prayer, Bible study and fellowship. The poor should be built into your life and circle of friends – not projects for the poor, but relationships with the poor. We will be richer when this is the case. Why? Because God commands us so. There are only three places where Jesus says he will meet us: in communion ('This is my body'[5]), in prayer and fellowship ('Where two or three gather in my name, there am I with them'[6]), and finally, when we engage with the poor ('Whatever you did for one of the least of these brothers and sisters of mine, you did for me'[7]). That is it. It is noteworthy that in all three we meet God when we are in relationship with others. We receive wine from another, we pray as a group and we meet God when we are with those in need. God commands us into community, and our religious rituals remind us of this and draw us into relationship. Being with the poor is a religious ritual. We will meet Jesus there.

Sometimes, though, to quote Mother Teresa, we meet the Lord in 'distressing disguises'.[8] However, these are still genuine experiences of encountering him. We don't want just to meet the risen triumphant Christ, because there was more to his life than that. His disciples witnessed him weeping, being attacked and abused, and experiencing such anguish that his sweat was like drops of blood. So don't be surprised if, when you are with the poor, you find you meet the Christ of Calvary: suffering, bruised, shamed and beaten.

Being a trustee of a charity and giving money to the poor are brilliant things to do. However, they are not quite the same as being personally involved. Being that one step removed may be contracting out your responsibilities to be in relationship with the poor. To repeat, you will be richer when you are with the poor. As I found through the insights I gained from meeting Krish, one's own spiritual walk might make a lot more sense too.

This point was neatly expressed in an email I received from one of our volunteers, Nigel, who runs the Hope into Action home in mid Sussex. He described his time helping a tenant there, a man called Grant:

> On reflection, my overwhelming feeling is that since becoming a Christian 30 years ago, I have never known God's presence more than I have during this journey, even through the really, really difficult days and nights: the desperate prayers that I and others have prayed that God has so faithfully answered; the breakthroughs at times that were so critical; God's unswerving assurance that he is in total control when

things looked such a mess; the Holy Spirit's rocket fuel at the times when I have been empty, exhausted and out of energy. The spiritual battle that we as a team have been fighting over Grant's life has been so real, life-changing and, I believe, life-saving . . . At times I've prayed with such fire! I've not prayed like this before, with a righteous anger. It has been good for my soul and broken me out of my conditioned, placid Christianity.

While my encounter with Krish brought memorable blessings, there have been rather more hair-raising experiences along the way.

28

'I'll come round and knife you'

Do all the good you can, by all the means you can, in all the ways you can, in all the places you can, at all the times you can, to all the people you can, as long as ever you can.

–Attributed to John Wesley

'Ask me that again and I'll come round and knife you!'

As well as heartbreak, we have also had challenge.

Mike was a nice guy – affable, polite and pleasant to be with. I enjoyed spending time with him as we moved him into our fourth house, the one we had bought with the money from the council. After I had got to know him, I spotted him in town one day as I was cycling along, and ended up giving him a 'backy' on my bike. He wasn't without his more difficult side, though: he had committed violent crime and was banned from seeing his former partner.

After a while, Mike was running behind with his rent. Central to the support package we offer is the requirement that tenants sign up and adhere to our rules and pay their bills. Challenging them when this is not done is part of our work. As Mike was late with his rent, I called him up and gently mentioned to him that he was behind with his payments.

Gruff with hostility and ablaze with anger, he told me in no uncertain terms that he would end my life if I were to make the same request again.

I was, needless to say, taken aback. Feeling both disempowered and a wee bit vulnerable, I hung up without saying a word.

I felt Mike probably just needed a bit of time to calm down. I wanted to trust him, to believe that I had just caught him on a bad day, and to follow my instinct that he was the good man I took him to be and that he wouldn't actually carry out his threat.

Still, in the corners of my mind, rational reaction still lurked. It would try to creep on to centre stage, and I would have to batter it back into the recesses, choosing to trust my deeper sense of who Mike really was.

Two days later, to his credit, he turned up and apologized.

Prior to his threat against me, I had needed to carry out an inspection of Mike's room. A bedroom is always, to some degree, a reflection of a person's life – and sometimes of his or her underlying chaos. Behind this hard man was a softer side. On the wall was a picture of his daughter, and then a Bible verse that said, 'I will soar on wings like eagles',[1] above a drawing of a golden eagle. Mike was a painter and decorator, and worked very hard in his trade. His trouble was controlling the urge to drink afterwards.

Some months after Mike threatened me, he was tragically found dead in his room. The coroner concluded that he had come back one night after having drunk too much and had choked.

Mike's mother was naturally distraught. As she planned the funeral, she asked if I would be able to speak at the service. In the speech, I quoted from Isaiah, the very verse that was on his wall. I like to think of Mike, far from perfect while on earth, now up above: soaring like an eagle, free from the chains of alcohol, able to look down and see the many people who loved him dearly.

In all our time, we've had very few violent incidents or threats, although there have been several other moments when things got a bit intense.

In our early days I had come to know one of our tenants very well – a man called Fred – and found him to be a real softy. However, I also knew that he could get into a truly foul mood. About three weeks after he moved out from our home, while he was battling with depression, I received a text from him threatening that he was going to stab me. I didn't really believe he would do it, so I decided to drive over to his flat to see what was wrong.

As I got out of the car, I realized it was possible I could be doing something very stupid, and found myself hoping I'd made the right judgement.

I made a quick call to a colleague: 'If you don't hear from me for a while, please check on me,' and then I rang the doorbell.

Fred opened the door and greeted me as though absolutely nothing had happened; there wasn't the slightest hint that he had sent the text. He just let me in.

Once inside, I could see the place was in a terrible state, so I got busy cleaning it up, and he joined me in the effort. After 30 minutes we had made a real dent on the mess. As I did the washing up and he helped with the drying, we stood side by side (rather than face to face) and he shared all he had been going through. We got him to the doctor, and he slowly came out of his depression.

Even with tenants who have been in jail, including those who committed violent crimes, I have rarely ever felt scared. I have seen them as human beings and treated them with respect and trust. In turn, 9 times out of 10 they return that favour; actually, make that 99 times out of 100. Even in the two situations I mentioned above, when I responded in love rather than by ramping up the rhetoric, I was able to continue the relationship after the threats.

Carl was one of those who had served a sentence for violent crimes. However, to those of us who got to know him, he was a likeable man. When he was released from prison, his church befriender, an older gentleman called Alan, met him off the train and took him to his new home.

Alan describes those first few weeks when Carl joined them:

We all put a lot into Carl. For the first few weeks, he had no money, no benefits, nothing. So the church saw to it that there was food in his fridge. Without us, even in those first two weeks, I doubt he would have stayed dry or out of trouble. He would have been living on the streets with absolutely no money. What would he have been supposed to do?

Three months after Carl had come out of prison, Alan came to me and said, 'Ed, I'd like to show Carl round the cathedral. Do you think that would be a good idea?'

It struck me as a very dull proposition, but, not wanting to offend, I gave an encouraging response.

Halfway around, at the back of the cathedral, Carl and Alan sat down together.

'Carl,' said Alan, 'we've got to know you now over the past three months. We can see you're a good lad, and my wife and I would like to give you our mobile numbers. We trust that you're not going to take advantage of us. We didn't want to give them to you when you first came out – for obvious reasons. Please call us whenever you want: you're like a son to us now.'

Carl, whose father had left him when he was still in nappies, was overwhelmed by this trusting gesture. That trip to the cathedral always held a special place in his heart, and he never did abuse the confidence placed in him.

After about 18 months of continued support and the building of relationships and trust – and that time frame is important – Carl had a job and was ready to move on. We stay in touch on social media, and every now and then have a coffee. I last saw him when he came to one of our events. By that stage he had been promoted from the factory floor and was managing 13 people. It was great to chat to him on an equal footing, manager to manager. I remember saying to him, 'People are people wherever they are; if you're managing people, you'll be having challenges. How are things going for you?' As we chatted, I could see his challenges were indeed of the same nature as mine.

We all loved working with Carl; he was so honest and so strong, and yet vulnerable at the same time. I don't like to monetize the work we do. I disagree with that approach on principle. Men and women are so valuable that you can't put a price on them or their progress or 'outcomes'. However, a lot of people in the sector do evaluate their work using a cost–benefit approach. I am fairly certain that without our support, Carl would have ended up back inside. That would have created court costs of tens of thousands of pounds, and prison costs of over £32,000 a year. In contrast, our costs are around £3,000 per tenant per year. We have consistently found that roughly 90 per cent of our ex-offenders do not go back to jail – a much higher reduction in recidivism than would otherwise be expected. Therefore, if one were to calculate our impact at a financial level, we have saved the Ministry of Justice millions of pounds.

We have also had a courtroom drama or two, where our tenants have been packed and ready to go to jail, but the judge has been so impressed by the work we have done and the engagement the tenant has made with us that, against all expectations, the tenants have avoided a custodial sentence. This has even happened with the judges known to be the harshest on the circuit. We suspect that people's prayers during the court hearings have had something to do with it. I remember one occasion when we had a tenant in court for growing illegal substances, and someone from my church told the judge, 'Your Honour, this guy is certainly a fool, but he is no criminal. He is also my friend, and it is my honest opinion it would not be right for him to go to prison.'

The judge chose not to hand down a custodial sentence.

Some may read this and think justice has not been done, and I understand that. We do believe in justice, and sometimes the best place for our tenants is jail. However, if one looks at the figures in our country, one can see that the revolving door of jail is too often a tragic cycle that is very hard to escape from. The

UK has one of the highest prison populations in Europe, with 150 inmates per 100,000 people, compared to 118 in France and a mere 81 in Germany. Prison numbers in the UK have increased from 45,000 in 1993 to over 85,000 in 2016. I don't think the 90 per cent growth is because we have suddenly given birth to more baby criminals. It reflects, at least in part, a change by successive governments towards greater custodial sentencing, with the courts sending more criminals to prison and imposing longer sentences. Does this work as a deterrent? Well, almost 70,000 people are released from jail every year, 46 per cent of whom are reconvicted within one year. The number for women is just a whisker lower, at 45 per cent (with 38 per cent having nowhere to go upon release). For those under 18, the level of returnees within a year rises to a shocking 69 per cent. If one calculates that each prisoner has four people who are affected by his or her imprisonment, then there are 340,000 people who feel a direct impact from the criminal justice system. That is almost one in every 200 in this country. I find that after most talks I give in churches, someone comes to me and tells me about a relative who is in prison or has recently been released.

The prison population disproportionately represents the poor of our nation: 15 per cent were homeless before entering prison; one in three has a mental or physical disability; half have the literacy levels of an 11-year-old. The vast majority of short-term sentences are for drug-related crimes, and more than half of prisoners have not committed violent offences. With prisoners costing over £32,000 per annum per individual,[2] it wouldn't cost much more to send them to a top private school like Eton!

Our prisons have become 'unacceptably violent and dangerous places', according to Peter Clarke, the Chief Inspector of Prisons.[3] In the year prior to June 2016 there were 17,782 prisoner-on-prisoner assaults, up 31 per cent from the previous year. Alongside this, rates of self-harming are at an all-time high.

Despite all this and the number of prisoners we work with, Mike's threat is the worst I have experienced in ten years of working with former inmates. We always try to see the best in people and believe in their potential, trusting in them and their innate desire to pull through. I truly believe that if one loves and respects people from one's heart, then, most of the time, they will respond well and respect you back. We have seen this over and over again as our churches have chosen to love rather than condemn.

29

Lengthening cords and strengthening stakes

Enlarge the place of your tent, stretch your tent curtains wide,
do not hold back; lengthen your cords, strengthen your stakes.
–Isaiah 54.2

By the summer of 2013, three years after our first home had opened, we had 16 houses running. Our staff and finances had grown to accommodate the expansion, but we were stretched. We were now managing well over £1,500,000 of housing stock and did not really have the financial gravitas our investors deserved. The trouble was we had no money to be able to pay someone with the expertise to oversee our finances.

I met up with two of our trustees, Gavin Bateman and Yvonne Emery, in the Bull Hotel in Peterborough to discuss the matter. After much conversation and exploring of dead ends, Gavin suggested that we advertise for a volunteer finance director to work two days a week. We all agreed it was a stupid idea, but why not do it anyway? We ended up with one applicant: Keith Nicholson, the former Finance Director of the Leprosy Mission, who was returning to work after a period of illness. Appointing him as a volunteer was one of the easiest human resources decisions ever made. Keith's wise guidance of our finances has steered us for the past six years. Now that his health is better, he is working for us as an employee.

We had also seen God's provision a year earlier in bringing us someone to work on the houses. It was obvious from early on that my handyman capabilities, limited as they were to paintbrush wielding, were no match for the task of refurbishing and running numerous properties. Just as the need became pressing, God brought us Noel Garner, who became our operations director and took over the responsibility of looking after our houses. He was a former builder, developer, town planner and chair of a housing association. He had just left the latter post and had been praying for some work that combined his faith, his compassion for the homeless, and his skills as a builder and developer. As well as his being a blessing to us, he also saw the opportunity as a blessing for him. He is a man of the highest integrity and has now been with us for seven years, looking after every house with absolute excellence.

I share these stories as they highlight how God has 'broken the bread' and continued to provide for us time and time again. There are countless other examples of situations where he has come through, in a period of austerity, to cause us to grow. We now have a staff of 29, and many of the new positions have been appointed before we had the necessary funds. This doesn't mean we couldn't do with more workers and that we aren't often stretched. Nor does it mean we appoint people willy-nilly (we put in strong processes and think hard about what we need). However, when we are convinced we need a new staff member, we go for it, while working out how to fund him or her.

Many charities rely on grants from government. I never wanted that because one ends up having to do what the government wants one to do, and I prefer to be free from such constraints. Obviously, we do work in partnership with, listen to and learn from other professionals in the sector. However, we are able to do things our way, and when their way contradicts our best thinking and our understanding of how God would want to care for people, we can choose what we feel is right.

Virtually all housing charities rely on rents significantly higher than ours – often double what we charge. One of the problems of charging high rents is that the tenants then make a rational choice not to get a job – because unemployment benefits cover housing costs. A person earning the minimum wage would have to work many hours per week to be no better off, after tax, than he or she would be 'on the dole'.

I have therefore never wanted to have high rents or to become reliant on rent as our sole source of income. We would then be in danger of sustaining unemployment, at which point our financial objectives would preclude us from achieving our social objectives. In that case, we would then effectively be running a business on the backs of the poor.

On the contrary, we incentivize work by giving bursaries to those who find it, and have increased our rents only once in ten years. We now have a turnover of over £1,000,000 and over 200 tenants sleeping in our homes every night – and have been able to do this while staying true to the above principles.

At the core of our financial model is a belief that Jesus can multiply the bread of finances to keep feeding the crowd. We find he does this in all manner of ways, using all manner of people. It is wonderful to watch his hands at work, bringing blessing and provision from unexpected sources through channels we have never imagined.

When I think about how God provides from all corners, I think of Joe, a homeless guy we housed in one of our homes in these early days. The words 'lovable rogue' fitted him better than anyone I have met. 'Rogue' because he would often get into trouble and was in and out of jail like a yo-yo, mainly for drug-related crimes due to a long-term addiction to cocaine and heroin. This had seen him spend the best part of seven years behind bars. 'Lovable' because, although in his late twenties, he had such puppy-like eyes and looked like a teenager, and in many ways acted like a child in need of affection. He was also heartbroken after social services took his child away from him and his partner; the pain of that separation gave further impetus to his drug use. At times, he would call or meet up with members from his church support team in tears as he battled to overcome the power of his addiction.

Joe landed a job as a decorator at a house that was being prepared for sale. He piped up and explained to the woman who owned it that we would make an excellent organization to sell it to. He'd pop into our office after work most days and bend my ear repeatedly about what a great house it would be for us.

'I'm sure it would, Joe,' I would reply time and again, trying to hide my exasperation, 'but we don't have any investors at the moment and so the chances are slim. Not only that, but we don't know any churches in the centre of town near the house, so the chances of this moving ahead are less than "very low".'

Each time we had this conversation, I'd hope that, this time, my explanation was sufficiently clear to get a reprieve.

A few days after I thought Joe had finally got the message, I received a phone call from the woman who owned the house. Evidently, she had gone to the same 'school of very persistent hard sells' as Joe. I tried my hardest to be polite, and managed to end the conversation (eventually) with the assurance that should an investor *and* a church come forward, I would immediately get back in touch.

Within two days of that conversation I received another phone call, this time from Jonathan Baker, the Canon of Peterborough Cathedral, asking if he could come for a visit. Jonathan was a highly respected Christian leader and had been a key player in the interfaith response to a nationalist march through town. He was, quite simply, an all-round great man. He arrived at our office and explained that, in an 'unusual confluence of circumstances' (he was also better educated than most in Peterborough), he had a family in his congregation who, due to a health breakdown, were now being evicted and were about to become homeless. At the same time, someone had come to him offering him an investment for a house.

Our annual report had landed on his desk just at that moment, and he wondered if I, perchance, had any houses that might be suitable.

Let me think.

Within a week we had looked around the woman's house, and she, Jonathan, the investor and I were sharing a coffee. It wasn't long before we had the property up and running. It was wonderful to see the impact on the evicted family. Instead of five of them living in a single room in a hostel, they had a proper home in which they could rebuild their lives. The three teenagers no longer had to walk four miles to school; instead they could take a short ten-minute walk in the mornings. The stability of the home enabled the father to regain his health and take on a job, after which they were able to move into a place of their own. Those children will always remember that the Church gave them a house when they were homeless.

That property has been used subsequently for a number of families and single mothers, including those fleeing violence and other horrific domestic situations. One of the tenants, Lisa, was a single mother whose husband had beaten her and her six children while struggling with addiction. When we first met them, all seven of them were living in one bedroom in a hostel, making do with just a microwave and kettle for catering. The house is now a home for a Syrian refugee family. It all came from the multiplying of bread or, put another way, the divine 'confluence of circumstances'.

And what about Joe, the lovable rogue? Well, he moved on from our house, remains in touch and has not been back to prison since we housed him. He is still lovable and, I suspect, has not entirely lost his roguish side.

30

To judge or not to judge

Love your enemies, do good to them, and lend to them
without expecting to get anything back. Then your reward
will be great, and you will be children of the Most High,
because he is kind to the ungrateful and wicked.

–Jesus in Luke 6.35

Not long after the house had opened with support from Peterborough
Cathedral, Jonathan Baker asked me to speak at a Wednesday
lunchtime service.

Standing up in the cathedral was quite a thrill, while being a
wee bit nerve-racking. The services are open to anyone, and visitors often sit in and listen. On this day there were probably about
60 people there, most of whom were retired – some of whom even
managed to stay awake during my talk.

I was given the title 'Love in Action' and spoke on a number
of things, including sharing one's wealth with the poor. I closed
on the theme of 'inviting the stranger into your home', drawing
on Matthew 25 (by welcoming the stranger you welcome Jesus)
and Hebrews 13 (by showing hospitality we may entertain angels
without knowing it). Both of these passages have a sense of a divine
encounter about them. I encouraged people to interpret these verses
in very practical terms, and suggested that inviting the homeless
into one's house is a profound statement of love, acceptance and
trust. I also mentioned that it could be a growth experience for
oneself as well. I shared that, even with three young children, Rach
and I had welcomed people who had been homeless to our house.
Of course, one should be wise and mindful of risks, but that should

not stop us obeying, in very simple and direct terms, the teaching of Jesus.

Afterwards, over the buffet, a woman challenged me about what I had said. 'Do you really think you should be encouraging people to invite the homeless into their houses?' she asked.

I politely defended my point but was careful not to offend. I discovered that she had been the wife of a vicar and was now a widow, and that she lived in Nottingham. The conversation was not heading towards consensus so we made excuses; she drifted off while I went to find another sandwich.

The conversation stuck in my mind, though. She must have been pondering it too because, in a strange 'confluence of circumstances', I happened to bump into her again, two weeks later in Nottingham train station, and she went back to the same topic. She was quickly on the attack again.

'You see, Ed, I just kind of think that, you know, I've worked all my life [serving the Church], and the homeless should also work. I don't think it's right for them to be lying around on the street.'

I listened, and then the time came for me to depart and I headed off. As I boarded my train, I remembered the words of the elder brother in Jesus' story of the prodigal son: 'All these years I've been slaving for you and never disobeyed your orders.'[1]

It occurred to me that for my new acquaintance, her good works had duped her into thinking she was of greater worth than the guys on the street. She had forgotten that she was also a dirty sinner in need of repentance; she had not understood she would meet Jesus at the table with her younger and prodigal brother. No doubt this vicar's wife had read the parable of the prodigal son dozens of times. Its full understanding, however, was yet a long way from her heart. Isaiah 58 informs us that *our* healing (not just the healing of those we look after) will quickly appear when we do away with the 'pointing finger'.[2]

A few days later, as I was still mulling over this lady's attitude, I was struck by the contrast of her outlook with that of a vicar friend of mine, Adrian Holdstock, as he met one of our tenants. I was sitting in Adrian's vicarage with Shane, a tenant who had, yet again, broken our rules. Shane had a violent past for which he had served time. He also struggled with alcohol, which did nothing to help with his tendency towards physical aggression. However, those of us who got to know him could see he was just a young boy at heart.

After we had talked through the consequences of his actions, we found that Shane opened up to us in a way that he hadn't previously in the ten months we had known him. Adrian asked sensitively about his father. Shane responded by explaining he knew nothing about his father; the best he could surmise, from the snatched conversations he had overheard and from the little his auntie knew, was that he was conceived in rape. His auntie remembered a night her sister went out and returned late in the early hours with her clothes in tatters. She had never spoken about what happened and was pregnant shortly thereafter. After Shane was born, his mother fell for another man, but unfortunately Shane did not get on with him as he grew up. As a result, he had left home at 14, convinced he could sort his life out by himself. He explained to us how he had carried shame all his life: the shame of not knowing his father, of believing he was a mistake, of having been conceived by an evil man in an act of violence. He was now in his late twenties and ready to admit that he was not able to sort his life out by himself.

We came to see how his relational poverty went right back to the moment of his conception.

Shane's sad story demonstrates all too well that it is not enough to look on the surface. It confronts us with the question of whether we are willing to take time to delve deeper and to put ourselves in another's shoes – and to do so even when they use those shoes to kick others. When we dig a bit deeper, we may find that behind certain types of behaviour is a cause that would break any individual. I hoped that if the vicar's wife had been there, she might have seen things differently by the end of the conversation.

Even without being there, or without such a sad background story, we are, in any case, called by Jesus not to judge. If I am honest, my more normal response is nearer to that of the vicar's widow – because my own good works, accumulated now over a long period of time, can harden my heart to the radical grace Jesus spoke of in his famous parable of the prodigal son. As such, I miss out on the extravagant celebratory party, where my younger brother – despite his association with prostitutes – is sitting next to my heavenly Father, drinking with him and eating meat from the fattened cow, while I remain, arms folded, in a grump outside.

To show that not all our stories end happily ever after, it was shortly after that day that Shane got drunk again and ended up being recalled to jail for a violent offence. Within hours of recall, he went to the prison chaplain and asked him to contact Adrian. Adrian visited Shane 48 hours later and had a very moving and open talk with him. If nothing else, Adrian, old enough to be his father, was giving Shane the advice, support and love he otherwise would not have had. His relational poverty had lessened just a little. I met him a week later and had one of the most real and honest conversations I have ever had with anyone.

We've lost contact with Shane now, but I like to think a little more light was shining into the dark areas of his heart, and maybe one day he will look back and remember how God was supporting him through some of his toughest times. In addition, both Adrian and I gained something from our meetings with Shane. Rather than sitting at a distance in judgement, we had the joy and privilege of eating with the prodigal. I like to think the Father was there also, because during our 'meal' my humanity and love grew in ways I can't really express. I know now that when my thoughts turn to Shane they go soft and, despite his violence and addiction to alcohol (which I obviously don't condone), I feel a fond love for him.

31

Expansion

God settles the lonely in families, he leads out the prisoners
with singing.

–Psalm 68.6

We had quickly found ourselves operational in four cities:
Peterborough, Cambridge, Norwich and Nottingham. One of the
big questions we faced was whether we should continue to expand
further. While we were thrilled about every opportunity, we were
struggling to raise money for salaries and were at full stretch; our
limited resources threatened to become a bottleneck to further
growth.

On the scene at the time was the concept of franchising.
'Franchising' is one of those words one hears a lot, but the truth is,
before I began Hope into Action, I had no idea what it meant. As I
researched it, I thought it fitted well with what we had to offer and
could enable our model to work in many more places.

However, the idea was not without its potential challenges. There
were concerns around whether our model, which is more complicated than most social enterprises, could work as a franchise. Could
we really get people around the UK to put hundreds of thousands
of pounds of capital into a melting pot, and then meld that with
church involvement and professional support?

After lots of discussion and research, we eventually decided that
the best way to find out if it worked was to test it.

We created an online manual in order to be ready to run with
the model. We had a lot of interest from people about the possibility
of setting up franchises, but as time went on, nothing materialized;

the manual wasn't much use without someone to implement it. I started to feel discouraged, and after a while I began to adjust my expectations. Perhaps we would just share our best practice; perhaps we wouldn't expand to other cities – that would be fine.

However, not long after formulating these thoughts, I was sitting in my office one afternoon when I received a call from a woman called Ardva in Lincoln. She told me that she loved our model and wanted to explore replicating it in Lincoln.

'Perhaps you could come down to Peterborough and we could discuss it further,' I proposed.

'Yes, that's exactly what I'd like to do.'

Turning to my calendar: 'When are you free?'

'How about tomorrow morning?'

And so at 9 a.m. the next day, there I was, sitting having coffee with Ardva. I was immediately struck by her dynamism and passion; she was a real go-getter and a natural leader, the sort of person you would definitely want on your side. Over the course of the conversation, she shared that she had been in the RAF and had subsequently held a senior role on Lincoln council. Her professional strength was beautifully married with a compassion demonstrated by her years of being a foster parent. It was a powerful meeting as we discussed how we would work together using a franchise model, and by the end of it we had begun formulating a plan that we could move forward with.

I came back with the good news, and the trustees agreed we should proceed with the franchise on a trial basis. As the cogs were now turning, we decided to draw in others who had expressed interest and invite them to an assessment day.

Among those who came was a bilingual lawyer from Wolverhampton called Matt Lambert. It didn't take long to see that Matt was a remarkable man with equally impressive quantities of presence and drive. As I got to know him, I realized these characteristics were combined with a sharp mind and an ability to turn his skills to almost any task – from fixing up a house, to writing proposals, to dealing with legal documents, to critiquing policy.

After Andy, Noel and I had formally assessed potential partners, we decided we would start new franchises with Ardva and Matt and then evaluate them after one year.

Matt and Ardva went ahead with setting up their own versions of what we do. They replicated the Hope into Action model without having to reinvent all the wheels and cogs, and we could expand without carrying the human resources, governance and fund-raising burdens for the houses.

Soon we had two new houses in both these new cities: the franchise was running and working well, homes were being created, and people were being housed and loved.

Matt and Ardva proved wonderful partners and excelled in their roles. Ardva worked day and night to bring the vision into reality. Matt did likewise, even to the extent that he gave up his legal practice to run the franchise.

Matt later went on to pioneer a new area of work for us that brought me a special joy and resolved an inner tension I had been carrying.

Alongside the amazing provision of homes and partners, we also saw God providing for us in the smaller details too.

A nice example of this happened in the early stages of Ardva's second house. She had finally got the home up and running, after investing all she had in terms of energy and finances, when one of her new tenants asked her for just one more thing: a pillow.

'We really have run out of money,' Ardva responded, 'but we can pray.' And that is what she did, right there and then.

That afternoon she received a phone call from a local hotel: 'We're getting rid of some pillows. Could you do with any?'

Over 70 pillows soon landed on her doorstep. Our tenants have been well 'pillowed' ever since.

We also saw this dynamic closer to home. While we had been expanding into other cities, our local work had been growing as well, and by this stage we had ten houses in Peterborough. I had come to realize that my decision to buy an electric scooter to get around between the houses had not been a good one. My staff and I concluded that what we actually needed was a car.

The only problem with this better decision was that we didn't have any money to implement it.

Sarah Vassiliades, then one of our part-time finance administrators, suggested that we might see if any of the local car dealers would have a suitable vehicle they could give us. I happened to have an old school friend called Jamie who worked for a car dealership, and I quickly pinged an email off to him on the off chance.

Later in the day when I opened my inbox, there was his reply:

Hi Ed,

Great to hear from you. Funnily enough, just this morning I was given the keys to a smart little van, which would probably be perfect for you. I was wondering what on earth we could do with it. Then, as I was thinking about it, your email popped through. So . . . how do you fancy it?

Jamie

We are still using that van to this day.

We have seen God's unmistakable hand in providing not only staff, investments, volunteers, pillows and cars, but also tenants.

We saw a wonderful example of this with Matt's work in Wolverhampton. Unexpectedly, Matt was approached by Youth For Christ about a young man called Nick who was on remand in Birmingham, awaiting sentencing. Like many inside, Nick's main concern about release was where he would live. However, release was more of a dream for him, and his greater fear was the looming custodial sentence of two to three years that was expected. He took his concerns to God in prayer.

While Nick was praying and waiting in the wings, Matt was running around getting a room ready for him just in case he was released. When Nick came before the court, the judge considered Matt's offer of housing and support and, to everyone's surprise, gave Nick a suspended sentence on the condition that he be accompanied straight back to the property. Matt waited at court until the evening when they had finally processed Nick, and then drove the young man to his new accommodation to enjoy a very different night's sleep from the one he had been expecting.

32

Shame

Shame is a soul-eating emotion.

–Carl Jung

We recognized that in implementing the franchising model we needed to ensure consistent quality. We wanted to be certain that all our Hope into Action homes, wherever they might be, would always have the same essential traits. Each home needed to be finished to a high standard, giving the tenants real dignity and showing them the true value of their worth, and it had to be run in conjunction with a church that welcomed and supported them, showing non-judgmental love.

We decided to monitor consistency by drawing up a questionnaire to capture learning, so that each tenant, and equally each church, would receive the same experience regardless of the home or city they were in.

I had the pleasure of sitting down with a tenant called Bill to ask for his input as I used the questionnaire for the first time in Lincoln. What started as a trial of a monitoring tool quickly turned around to be a meaningful and personal encounter with a special and tender-hearted man.

Bill was one of our first tenants in the city and was a gentle soul. He had been sleeping rough and selling *The Big Issue* before we met him.[1] He was what you might call a natural victim and so found the streets an aggressive place where people pushed him off the best pitches. He enjoyed his spliffs (not in our houses, though), and no doubt this contributed to a fragile state of mental health. Once in the church home, however, he met the warmth of people who didn't push him out of the best pews on a Sunday morning. It was a small congregation, which worked for him as he was a shy person and might have been intimidated by the bigger crowds at other churches. He soon volunteered for the church and became a regular member of its homegroups and Sunday worshipping community.

The questionnaire was more like a guided conversation, and it allowed the topics to roll and move if appropriate. Bill shared with me how he was estranged from his mother; she had rejected him at a young age and now lived far away in New Zealand. He was desperate to be in touch with her and expressed his gratitude for the help we had given him in that area.

The conversation was warm and open, with him asking me questions, which I happily answered. At the bottom of the form we had included some 'diversity' questions to track ethnicity, gender, age and other characteristics, and the final question was about sexuality. I really didn't want to ask it, but I eventually decided that since we were trialling the questionnaire, we wouldn't know if it worked unless I did.

So I asked Bill to confirm his sexuality and read out a list of options.

There was a pause.

'I'm heterosexual . . . I think. I always get those terms muddled up. I like girls – that's right, isn't it?'

'Yes,' I replied as I ticked the appropriate box, already feeling this question was a bit intrusive. (I don't ask it now.)

He then continued. 'I can't understand why anyone would want to do it the other way.'

Further awkwardness. How do I reply? 'Erm, well, I'm of the same persuasion . . . '

'I remember once when I was thirteen and I was walking home through the park. It was dark and . . . '

I need not fill you in on all the details, but he then disclosed, with some intimacy, how he had been raped.

I was surprised he would share such a thing with me so freely and appreciated his trust.

While Bill was unusually open (and probably too trusting of people he had barely met), our guess is that many keep such events hidden. It is hard to admit to them.

Whether disclosed or not, all too often the impact cannot be hidden. I think of a former tenant, Charlene, a bubbly, pretty young woman, who reappeared in our office one day and shared that she had been raped. Before, she had had so much spirit; now she looked like just a shell of a person. It was as though something inside her had died.

We don't know how many people have suffered such abuse. Our guess is that over 90 per cent of our female tenants have experienced some form of sexual violence, and a good percentage of our male tenants too. Even some of the 'hard ones' have admitted as much to me.

I am no expert on how to respond. However, after a conversation I had with an old family friend, Rebecca Winfrey, I began asking myself about the difference between guilt and shame. Rebecca was studying shame for a theological dissertation. I came to realize I didn't know the difference between shame and guilt. My guess is that most Christians couldn't articulate it either.

'Victims of abuse', argued Rebecca, 'will often suffer shame – but they are not guilty.' As Fossum and Mason put it in their book *Facing Shame*: 'While guilt is a painful feeling of regret and responsibility for one's actions, shame is a painful feeling about oneself as a person.'[2]

Guilt is a fairly straightforward emotion to understand. When your mother is not looking, you hit your brother. He cries. He tells Mum. You feel guilty (or feign a sense of guilt). You then need to ask for forgiveness. Once that is granted, relationships are restored. I learned that in Sunday school, and I imagine most ten-year-olds could explain it. It is seismically 'good news' and is also quite easy to grasp.

Shame, Rebecca began to show me, is different. I began reading books on the subject to understand it more. Someone who has been raped or abused, or grown up surrounded by abuse, might well feel a profound sense of shame. Yet that person has done nothing wrong.

Clearly, if after Bill told me he had been raped, I had replied with the words: 'Don't worry, you are forgiven', that would have been both patently absurd and highly damaging. He clearly didn't need to be forgiven for being a rape victim as it wasn't his fault. (In the three instances of sexual violence in the Old Testament, you will not find one hint of blame towards the victim.) Yet the attack would have affected him deeply.

The odds are that those who have suffered abuse have already heard it was their fault, or felt as though it was. Abusers will often – sometimes subtly, sometimes deliberately – blame the victim. They will make the innocent person feel that he or she is to blame. My worry is that sometimes our Christian narratives might, subconsciously, reinforce that false sense of guilt. Alongside not implying guilt, we should also be careful that others do not receive that message through their own filters.

For those who carry shame, the message of the need for forgiveness may need a little tender thought. An overemphasis in our liturgy, prayers and songs on forgiveness might serve to deepen this embedded sense of shame and unhealthy guilt.

We may therefore need to tread sensitively when we discuss forgiveness. It is true that we are all called to forgive, based on the command and example of Jesus. However, if the only message the victims hear, especially in an ongoing situation, is to forgive others, that could serve the interest of the victimizer by pacifying the victim and exposing him or her to further harm. Forgiveness should not give any validity to what was done. It does not relieve the perpetrators of responsibility for what they have done; nor should it erase accountability. With this preface, we can talk about forgiveness (sometimes, though, much later) and about its power to bring healing to the cancer of bitterness or hatred that can take root in the soul.

I began to notice as I read the Gospels that Jesus didn't tell everyone he met to repent or that they needed to be forgiven. Think of the bleeding woman, or the criminal dying on the cross next to him.[3] In neither case does Jesus even mention sin.

How, therefore, do we respond to sufferers of shame, and what do we say to those who have been humiliated? What is our 'good news' response to a deep sense of shame?

The bleeding woman was a person who, like the abused, had done nothing wrong. It wasn't her fault she was bleeding. Yet society had ostracized her for it. She would have suffered great shame for many years for something that was not a sin. Jesus did not say to her 'Your sins are forgiven', as he said to the paralysed man whom he'd met a little earlier in the Gospel narrative.[4] I've often wondered why he didn't. Perhaps doing so would have compounded her sense of shame. Even as she admitted her ailment and suffering to Jesus, we can almost hear the whispering crowd condemning her: 'Dirty woman – what's she doing here?' 'She's unclean.' 'How dare she?' 'Look at her filthy rags.' 'I would never be out if I was in that condition.' 'Stop bothering this man – he has an important work to do with someone of greater worth than you.' Stigmatizing her. Shaming her. Silencing her.

Before his encounter with the bleeding woman, Jesus had been on his way to the home of a synagogue leader who had asked him to heal his dying daughter. Jesus must have felt strong peer pressure to deal with the critically ill child over the chronically suffering adult; the important religious ruler over the reject; the law over love; the glamorous over the gory; the clinical simplicity of a child's healing over the uncomfortable issue of this woman with her bloody rags. But he stopped. He listened. In front of everyone, he affirmed her. He claimed her as his own: 'Daughter.' He praised her: 'your faith has healed you', and he liberated her: 'be freed from your suffering.' It is noteworthy that the tenses are different in the two statements. If the accomplished healing (in the past tense) referred to her bleeding, perhaps the present and future freedom referred to some suffering other than the physical – maybe a deeper suffering, such as that of being shunned by society, or of shame. He blessed her: 'Go in peace.' Be at peace with God and at peace with society, because – remember – whatever they say, your identity is wrapped up in being my daughter.[5]

Jesus didn't mention this woman's sins. She needed wholeness. Many on the streets need the same.

33

Billionaires can come in unexpected guises

All the animals of the forest are mine, and I own the cattle on
a thousand hills.

–Psalm 50.10 NLT

It was Easter 2014 and I was away with my family on a short break.
I had awoken early; the air was still cool and I felt at my best, as I
often do in the mornings. I found my mind filling with thoughts
about how Jesus had always been there for those in need. As I
scanned the story of the gospel, I felt I had something fresh to add
to the talk I would give at Life Church in Peterborough later that
day.

Life Church was aptly named, and as I entered to a warm and
vibrant welcome, I could feel vitality and energy oozing from the
congregation. It was the perfect place to share the thoughts that had
been building since my early morning musings.

I spoke about how Jesus, from his birth to his death, was always
there for people who felt rejected by the world and by religious
leaders. He was there for the shepherds, the foreigners, the vulnerable individuals who appear in almost every encounter in the
Gospels, and even those present at the cross.

I highlighted that the theme 'from birth to death' can also be
applied to the way the Gospels elevate women. I mentioned how
much the words of Mary and Elizabeth are recorded in Luke. The
first ever missionary? A female divorcee. Another Mary and her
sister, Martha, told not to worry about housework. A prostitute.

An adulterer. In Jesus' stories the women are always cast as heroines, and the villains are always men. On the cross, he cares for his mother. The first person to be trusted with the gospel after his resurrection? Another woman. Four books written by four men, about a fifth man, in a highly patriarchal society, and there is not even one derogatory comment about a woman.

I then explained how we seek to reflect these themes through the work of Hope into Action. A couple of our tenants were with me, and one shared his story: a story of how he had been wealthy but fell homeless, and how the Church had met him at his point of greatest need.

After the service, I was touched to see how warmly everyone responded to the tenants. As I watched somebody give one of them a hug, I noticed a man approaching me wearing shorts, a Superman hooded top and flip-flops. Here we go, I thought. Brace yourself.

The man, whose name was John, asked me some questions, and I quickly realized that, despite his attire, he seemed to have a rather sharp mind.

My second impression proved to be right; he turned out to be a top civil servant in one of the major ministries in London.

His sharp mind was complemented by a tender humility, and the Holy Spirit seemed to have stirred his compassion as he listened to the testimony of our tenant. 'I think I might be able to introduce you to someone who may just be able to help,' he said as he handed me his card.

When I followed up, John shared with me that he had done a lot of work with a billionaire property owner called Samuel. I should probably use the word 'mogul', but I've never quite understood the exact point at which someone passes into that category.

A few months later, John, Gavin Bateman and I were sitting in the reception area of Samuel's office in central London. It was smart and well set out, though not obviously ostentatious. I had spent the previous evening researching Samuel's profile. He was on the

Sunday Times Rich List and, as far as I could tell, owned half of central London.

After some nervous fidgeting as we waited, we were ushered into an office, where Samuel greeted us warmly and cordially. He exuded an air of self-assured confidence that stopped short of the arrogance one might expect from someone of such wealth. Taking the lead naturally, he politely asked me to describe what I did. After I had explained myself, he responded, 'Well, you can't earn a million pounds from that. How much do you get?'

I replied that I earned around £30,000. He'd sized me up. It didn't appear he thought I'd made much of a career choice.

We carried on talking for another 15 minutes or so, and then he finished by suggesting we should meet his brother Daniel, who ran their foundation.

Two months later, Noel and I met up with Daniel. We were very impressed with him, finding him to be humble, a good listener and keen to help.

We have developed a valued relationship with Daniel. The two brothers belong to an incredibly generous family and that generosity has been directed towards our work, as well as many other worthy causes. Over a period of years they have also bought four houses, which they own and lease to Hope into Action on a 'peppercorn rent'. I didn't know what that legal term meant when they first used it and so had to ask a solicitor.

'It's an old term,' I was told. 'It means a token or nominal rent charged when the owner of a property wishes to lease it for free. Literally it means that at any stage in the future, they can ask you for a peppercorn as rent and you have to give it to them.'

'Ah. Okay. Thanks.'

I put down the phone and went out to find a peppercorn shop.

Samuel wasn't the last billionaire I was to meet – though my experience with the next one was to be altogether different.

34

Disappointment and joy go hand in hand

> We love our people whether they turn out well or not and the
> successes do not vindicate our ministry nor the disappoint-
> ments nullify it. What is important is whether we have loved
> in a real way – not preached in an impassioned way from a
> pulpit.
>
> *–Jackie Pullinger,* Chasing the Dragon, *1980*

At this time, I was getting a lot of phone calls from people interested
in what we were doing. The calls could come from anywhere across
the UK, and I never quite knew which ones would work out and
result in a house.

One of these enquiries came from a woman called Tara from
an ancient market town in the heart of one of the beautiful home
counties. As I wasn't sure whether the connection would lead
anywhere, I scheduled the call for a time when I was driving to
Milton Keynes (a hands-free call, of course!). It turned out to be
a longer chat than I had anticipated, and I ended up steering my
way simultaneously through the conversation and the hundreds of
roundabouts in Milton-everything-looks-the-same-Keynes!

Tara explained that she had a friend whose daughter, Frances,
had fallen into drugs, then into addiction, then into crime and
eventually into prison. Tara had committed to help her friend and
regularly drove to London to visit Frances in jail.

Frances had got clean while in prison and wanted to return
to her home town, but she was anxious not to end up in a hostel.

Tara, whose big heart was clearly matched by admirable drive and passion, was looking for alternatives and had come across Hope into Action during her online research.

We chatted over our model and I invited her to our first ever conference, not really expecting her to come.

However, when the day of our conference arrived, there was Tara. Not only did she make the conference; she also made the decision to set up a house.

She found a church to partner with, and we all agreed to go ahead with setting up a women's house. However, when we got down to the nitty-gritty of the proposal, the church leaders struggled with the idea of accepting people of all sexualities. We did not feel the partnership was going to work, so we blessed them and went our separate ways.

Indomitable, Tara went off and found another church, this time a church with a strong community focus and a leader so keen to be involved that he came to visit me in Peterborough.

I sensed this project would have legs, so I arranged a return visit even though there was still no sign of an investor on the horizon.

'Don't worry,' I confidently asserted to Tara. 'This is often the way. Trust me, it's harder to find a church than an investor. Let's keep moving it forward in faith.' (Strangely, this is true. We ask churches for seven to ten people who are prepared to build relationships with the tenants, and we ask an investor to provide enough money to purchase a house. We often have more investors than churches willing to commit their resources.)

By the time I arrived we had found an investor – someone able and willing to buy an entire house for us. Amazingly, that is often how it happens, and it feels like a miracle every time. It also meant I could arrive with a smug look on my face as if to say, 'I told you so – what were you worried about?' As part of our schedule, we met the investor to go over the details, and then Tara drove me round and showed me that behind the famous tourist frontage of her town were dens of depravity unseen by most visitors, and even many residents.

Tara was keen that Frances should be assessed independently of her. So one cold January day, I caught the train down to London to visit Frances in prison. I met up with a church volunteer called Louise, who had also travelled a long way to be there. After being told to take half our clothes off, we finally made it through security – with our clothes now back on. Only then were we told that Frances was refusing to meet us. Bummer. We'd both invested the best part of a day in making the trip. My new friend, Louise, told me to pray. So I did, under my breath, without moving my arms, or my feet – or even my lips. Meanwhile, Louise marched up and down the austere prison corridor speaking loudly in tongues. She was slightly bolder than I was.

Something worked, because within five minutes we were sitting in front of Frances.

After some small talk, I asked Frances what had happened that had led to her being in prison. She responded by telling us about her crimes.

'And now tell us why you're really here.' It's not a line I have used before or since, but it seemed to work.

Frances looked down nervously at first, but after a while she lifted her eyes to meet ours, as we all held the silence. Slowly, her shoulders dropped and she leaned in a little as she started to speak. As she opened up, she took us back with her, right to the root of where it started: the day she had been in her bedroom with her first boyfriend and he had raped her. 'I felt awful about it,' she said mournfully. 'I didn't know who to talk to. I didn't want to tell my mother because I felt so ashamed.' Long pause, as she gathered herself: 'Anyway, within a few months I had met another man and after a while I told him what had happened. He introduced me to a fantastic coping mechanism: heroin. By the age of sixteen I was addicted.'

The air now felt heavy. Frances continued her story, sharing with us how, in the intervening ten years, she had had a child and then later been sentenced to two years. Now she was coming to the end of that term, and she had managed to get clean of drugs.

She finished and looked me in the eye: 'I can honestly say to you I am really proud of where I am.'

I was so struck by the tragedy of her story that I replied, 'Yes. You should be. You've shown amazing courage.'

And it was true: she should be proud. I truly felt enormous admiration for her. To some she may have been a failed mother, a recovering addict and an offender – and to a certain degree she was all of those things. Yet she was also an incredibly courageous woman who had done so well to get clean and be where she was.

'Five minutes,' we heard the guard intone.

Where had those 45 minutes gone? Louise and I quickly excused ourselves and left the room to confer and make a rapid decision. We were both so moved and inspired that we felt we had to give her the home. We went back in and Louise broke the news. Frances wept with relief and joy. We ended in hugs.

Frances also shared how anxious she was about being homeless for any period of time, and in God's amazing timing (and with one heck of a lot of effort by the church) we had the new house open and ready (just) on the day she was released. As Tara went to collect her, the rest of the team finished the decorating and got the welcome pack ready.

The volunteers settled Frances into the home, but the early weeks were full of practical challenges for her, as Tara describes:

On release there are many difficulties facing the ex-offender. I had known Frances for years, and I could see the transition from prison had left her disorientated. The benefit money took over three weeks to come in. How was she supposed to pay for the electricity and gas meters – not to mention food or the bus to get to probation appointments? It takes so much time and energy, and a fair amount of intellect or education, to get all this sorted out. This is where the mentors from church really stepped in. We helped her set up bank accounts for the benefits to go into and sourced food and a week's start on the meter. We helped with lifts to the probation office as there was no money to buy a bus card – and in any event it couldn't have been arranged in time. Without that support I just don't see how anyone could have coped and stayed within the boundaries of the law; it's just such a difficult transition.

For the first few weeks Frances did really well. She met up regularly with mentors and took responsibility for making decisions, getting to appointments, paying her bills and taking control of her life again. However, things started to slip as her old habits crept back in. Appointments were missed, rules were ignored, drugs were found in her room and known dealers were coming to the house.

Tara again:

It was so disappointing to watch the decline, and we continued to try to reach her, but drugs had got hold of her again. It ended with too many missed probation appointments and too much chaos, and she was recalled to prison. I was gutted and not a little battered emotionally.

After her difficult experience with Frances, Tara shared, 'I, somewhat weirdly, felt the desire to pray for someone who had been in slavery. I don't know why; I think I was so bruised by Frances that I wanted someone different.'

Not long after Tara had prayed this, her vicar, Robert, got chatting to someone who mentioned she had a homeless woman from the Far East sleeping on her sofa. She told him this person, whose

name was Kanya, had fled from a town in Wales with no possessions – she had absolutely nothing. Robert's attention was piqued,
and in no time he and Tara were visiting Kanya.

As they sat together, Kanya shared with them that she had
suffered a stormy and abusive upbringing. Her mother had been
unable to care for her due to alcohol and drug addictions, and she
had been put into foster care at the age of four. She then suffered
terrible abuse at the hands of her foster parents. When, as a teenager, she eventually summoned up the courage to report what was
happening, she was just thrown back into the foster care system.
By that stage she was suffering with severe mental health issues.
She tried to continue her education but, without family or financial
support, could not get to university. She then met a woman who
befriended her and introduced her to a man whom she described as
her uncle. He promised Kanya a job and a better life in the UK. She
gratefully accepted the offer of help and followed the instructions to
meet at the airport in the capital to travel together.

The dream job turned into Kanya's worst nightmare. Her pass-
port was taken from her and she was trafficked – forced into
prostitution as a sex slave, drugged, and moved all over the UK. She
endured unimaginable suffering and thought she was going to die
on a number of occasions. In the end, her captors decided to sell her
to human organ traffickers for £10,000. She gathered all her courage
and fled when the opportunity arose. She ran as fast as she could
and managed to get to the police.

Tara and Robert were cut to the heart as they listened to Kanya's
story and her devastating experiences. They both immediately
wanted to help her and to offer her a home.

A few days later I was sitting in my office, away from the emotion
and immediacy of Kanya's situation, reviewing their assessment
forms with some degree of trepidation. Would she cope? Surely she
was too 'high need' for us. Could the church handle someone with
such a background?

I shared my concerns with Tara and Robert, questioning whether we could manage such a serious need. However, they were not to be swayed, and as they had met her and were the best informed, I needed to trust their judgement for the final call.

Two weeks later Kanya was no longer sleeping on the sofa; instead she had a home she could call her own.

Tara and her team welcomed Kanya with open arms and invested many months of hard work, faithful love, persistent prayer and sacrificial time in looking after her.

Over to Tara:

Kanya came to us as an incredibly troubled young woman. However, the difference was that she was able to maintain her desire to get help and interact, and was able to keep the house rules. She was an absolute delight to work with, love and befriend.

There were huge challenges along the way. We had many suicide attempts, a lot of self-harming, including self-harming by drinking herself into oblivion, especially when important dates like Christmas and birthdays came around.

However, she always survived, as did the team, and we carried on loving her. When she found a female partner we stood alongside her in that relationship, and we were also there for her when that broke down.

Kanya needed a lot of help accessing mental health support and would not have been able to do this on her own. She finally got an appointment and we helped her get there, both physically and emotionally. Her desire to avoid it was huge as it hurt so much to talk about the past traumas. Our support worker was enormously helpful in setting everything up and putting things in place. The medication in this instance worked. She got a new medicine, and the self-harming and suicide attempts virtually stopped.

Months later, an opportunity came for Kanya to move some-where with specialist counselling, and she was strong enough to do so. Tara and the team keep in touch, and she is doing really well. Nothing is plain sailing, but she continues to face her challenges with wisdom. On the way, she has found a quiet, private faith, won awards for her resilience and been on television to speak about trafficking.

Tara again:

Kanya was an absolute delight to work with, even though it was emotionally shattering! The difference here is that she desperately wanted the help and the option of a new life, so she put in the effort to make the changes needed. Frances, unfortunately, was drawn back into her old life and didn't have that inside strength needed for change . . . yet!

The journey of life for both Frances and Kanya continues to have its hurdles and heartaches. We keep in touch with both of them. My heart soared recently when Kanya wrote:

When I think back, I am amazed at what my life looks like today. I have been through such dark times – when I felt so utterly alone and scared, without hope or any way forward, when I was trapped and surrounded by cruelty. But now I have life, hope and happiness. I am so grateful for all those who have been there for me – sometimes when there was no reason for them to be the ones to stand by me – but they did. They were there to hold me, to take my hand as I walked through the hardships and processed my heartbreak. They were there for me when I needed practical support or a shoulder to cry on. They gave me hope when all I could see was darkness. Now my heart is mending and my mind is healing. I am able to enjoy life and the relationships around me. I am so glad that they have been there for me and helped bring me out to this safe and happy place that I am now enjoying. I never imagined I would feel so at peace and so happy as I do today.

Trafficking is a tragedy. Kanya's is but one story of a survivor of this terrible crime. There are thousands more in the UK alone. We now have one house caring purely for survivors of trafficking. However, the nation needs many more. It is estimated that half of the victims of trafficking in this country return to homelessness within six months of leaving a safe house. We need far more places that can carry such people through the long course of recovery. Survivors need a home in which they can try to make sense of their past and begin to relaunch their future.

In the comfort of the average church pew, these are issues that don't often demand a practical response, but in our job the need continues to smack us in the face. It gets in among us, unseats our complacency and drives us out to help others who are still entangled in the gruesome web of terror that trafficking spins around its victims.

I have shared both Kanya's and Frances's stories because I think together they give a good feel for who we are. Both women would be classed as 'high need' by us; both would be 'risks'. While we perform lots of needs, strength and risk assessments, ultimately everyone we move into one of our homes is a risk. You never know quite how a person will turn out. We need to be wise and to learn (and we often tell our people not to let their heart rule their head), but at the end of the day we are fundamentally risk-takers.

It is tempting to focus on telling the testimonies of those who have made significant turnarounds – and, trust me, we have plenty more of those we could share. We also have many such testimonies that we will never tell because we have been asked not to, and the needs of our tenants supersede our need for a good story. However, in sharing outcomes both encouraging and disappointing, I want to show that outcome is not the barometer of success.

We know that in some cases our investment in a tenant's life will bring tremendous reward, while in others it will bring much hurt. But we love anyway.

Triumph and tragedy. Joy and sorrow. We accept both as part of the journey. Our job is to show love. That, in fact, is how we define our success. Have we shown love? Has the tenant felt and received love? If so, we have succeeded. We have no power over what he or she does with that love. To quote Jackie Pullinger: 'The successes do not vindicate our ministry nor the disappointments nullify it. What is important is whether we have loved in a real way.'[1] In both the above cases we were equally successful – because we and the church strove to love each person as best we could.

35
Office move

My people will live in peaceful dwelling-places, in secure homes, in undisturbed places of rest.

–Isaiah 32.18

In the autumn of 2014 I received a phone call from our landlord asking us to vacate the office in Peterborough city centre. We had now been in there three years and we loved it. Luckily they didn't give us a strict time frame in which we had to move out, as it turned out we couldn't find anywhere else to go. We looked around a whole raft of properties, from disused pubs to formal offices above shops, but they all proved to be too expensive or unsuitable for some other reason. We also discovered that reputable estate agents don't want to have a homeless charity as tenants. Neither do disreputable estate agents.

A few months into our search, we held a trustees' meeting to examine all the options. Midway through a tedious discussion on interest rates, budgets and rental prices, Andy piped up, ''ang on – 'ave we prayed into this yet?'

I groaned inwardly; the last thing we needed just as we were trying to work through an important detail was some hyper-spiritual 'holier than thou' comment.

Nevertheless, we acquiesced.

We decided to pray and fast about the situation on 5 January 2015, and on that day Andy led us in a lunchtime of prayer. From that time on, we all felt a lot more at ease, and we also started exploring other options.

At the end of that month I was walking through Cathedral

Square when I received a call from David, my minister. It was rare for him to call me, and I had a sense that it was bad news.

'Ed, there is no easy way of saying this.'

(Uh oh.)

'Andy has died. I've just been on the phone to his wife.'

My mind reeled as I took in the shock.

For the next few days I felt as though my head was immersed in fog as I struggled to come to terms with the news. I took off to the cathedral to read and think.

As I mulled over who Andy was, I wrote these words:

As prison chaplain to HMP Peterborough, Andy was a passionate supporter of all we stand for, and was one of the core group who set up Hope into Action, and a trustee. Andy possessed an incredible gift for helping people who found themselves on the edge of society.

Servant of the church, fighter of injustice, friend of the poor. 'Rivers of living water flowed within him.' He was also a husband, a father and a grandfather, and is greatly missed.[1]

On the day of the funeral the church was packed to the rafters, with former prisoners and prison officers grieving alongside Andy's wife of 39 years, his three children and many other family members, all of whom loved him dearly, just as he had loved them.

It was evident that Andy was much loved and greatly missed.

The words I had written were included in his funeral and now hang on the wall of our new office, alongside a picture of him.

Andy left a huge gap in our work. I missed him, and his passion and gifting. We wanted to find a way to honour Andy and the incredible legacy he had left in so many lives and in Hope into Action itself. We felt it would be a fitting tribute to establish an annual Andy Lanning Award to recognize a tenant who had made a particularly amazing turnaround.

Eight weeks later, on the day of our conference, it was a poignant tear-filled moment as Andy's son, Gareth, presented the first Andy Lanning Award. Gareth has presented the award every year since, and it is always an emotional and special moment.

It took a while after Andy's death to find the energy to refocus on the search for the office.

However, after we had picked ourselves up from the shock, we recommenced the quest in late February. It was still a struggle, as one lead after another took us to a dead end. Nevertheless, through it all, I felt a lot more peace than I had in our original search.

After a while, though, as the weeks dragged on, I found the process was getting me down again, and I resolved to pray into the need, which I did on the Sunday before Easter.

The next day, one of our staff members, Duncan, mentioned there was a place for sale on North Street. As I looked at the property online, my interest was piqued: could this finally be what we were looking for? We got in touch with the agent, and Noel and I visited the property the next day. It had 12 good-sized rooms and was finally a space we could imagine working for us. The next day I put in an offer, and a day later we had agreed terms at £265,000. The place needed a complete refurbishment, including a new roof, plumbing, electrics, data points, a full repaint and a new kitchen. All this would cost an additional £90,000. The only issue was that we had no money and no guarantee of a mortgage. Without a deposit, the only way it could work was for an investor to come up with an initial £100,000. With nothing on the horizon, we decided to move ahead in faith, hoping that an investor would approach us. Keith scoped out the potential mortgage companies without informing them we didn't actually have a deposit at all yet.

Amazingly, an investor did come through with £100,000, and we got a mortgage.

It fell to Noel, as Operations Director, to supervise the refurbishment. By September I was getting a bit worried as no real work had begun on the property, but I was trying not to say anything and show that I trusted Noel. During a meeting, one of the staff asked him when we would move in, and he replied that it would be by the end of October. We fell about laughing. No one expected that to be the case. However, by the end of October, Noel had sequenced all the contractors perfectly and refurbished the property completely from roof to floorboards, electrics to plumbing, and carpets to painting. You name it, Noel had fixed it (or more accurately, had got someone else in to fix it). He oversaw everything in the refurbishment, and it really was a joy to watch him make so many amazing decisions to such good effect.

We now own a property that is just five minutes' walk from Peterborough station and that we bought completely with borrowed money. On top of that, the combined ongoing costs are less than they would have been if we had rented a space half the size. At times, the wait tested our faith, but now I am so thankful that we have such spacious accommodation, acquired at such a low price.

36

Our deepest fear

Our deepest fear is that we are powerful beyond measure.

–Marianne Williamson

By the time we moved into our office, we had 35 houses and over 70 tenants. Jesus kept multiplying those loaves. The story of each of those new houses could fill pages and pages of text, with thousands and thousands more words. (I haven't even mentioned our home for former sex workers, apparently the only transition house for ex-prostitutes in England, according to a researcher who interviewed me about it.)

I am reminded of the bizarre and confusing words with which John ends his Gospel: 'Jesus did many other things as well. If every one of them were written down, I suppose that even the whole world would not have room for the books that would be written.'[1]

Every time we open a new house and every time we enter a new town and every time we take a significant step of expansion, I feel scared once again. What on earth are we doing? How will we support the work? What about the finances? At these challenging moments, someone will invariably ask me a question about how fast we are growing, as if to say, 'Are you really sure that's wise?'

I remember wrestling with such worries on my way to the leaving service of Jonathan Baker, the well-educated Canon of Peterborough Cathedral and one of the loveliest and best-respected Christian leaders in Peterborough. I was unable to make the beginning of the service as I had a prior commitment, so I arrived midway through Jonathan's sermon, just as he was saying, 'Jesus said, "Put out into deep water and let down the nets."'[2]

Yes. This was the message and reassurance I needed. We love to cuddle Jesus as a safety blanket, but he calls us out of safety. He calls us, as he did his disciples in Mark 4, 'to the other side' – to the other side of the lake, to the other side of our society. Out of the shallows (and shadows). Into the deep. Following him is not safe; we will experience fear. If we want to see new lands, we have to consent to losing sight of the shore. Be certain of this: on the journey of Hope into Action I have made a thousand and more mistakes and bad decisions. The temptation is to step back and withdraw, crippled by negativity and awareness of our failings. However, this is not what Jesus has called us to. He calls us to lift our eyes up, to look outwards, to see again the immensity of the vision he has given us, to 'go and make disciples of all nations'.[3]

At times, the scope of what Jesus calls us to collides with my inner conditioning of Christian humility and false modesty. He repeats, time and again, the words 'Do not fear'. Some of those fears are more hidden than others. I was unaware of one of the most restraining and insidious fears that can affect me until I came upon a text by Marianne Williamson called 'Our Deepest Fear'. In it she pinpoints: 'Our deepest fear is that we are powerful beyond measure.'[4]

Paradoxically, sometimes my biggest fear can actually be a fear of success and growth. I don't like that word 'success'. I have all sorts of theological questions about it: some of those questions will be valid; others won't. Between the lines of our story are many personal failures and bad decisions that I have made (and not let you know about). However, we also put our head above the parapet and celebrate our 'success' so we can give glory to God.

If we remain in him, I trust we will continue bearing 'much' fruit. For, as Jesus said, 'This is to my Father's glory, that you bear much fruit, showing yourselves to be my disciples.'[5]

Fear is quick to pounce when we sense opportunity. When we feel stirred, however faint that stirring might be, it is good to act.

God gives us the opportunity to show our faith by letting us take that first step. If we don't step out, it won't be faith. We find that when we take that first step, God steers us as we move forward.

From time to time, when new vistas seem daunting or I am hesitating to step out, I will go back to Marianne Williamson's quote: 'Our deepest fear is that we are powerful beyond measure.'

37

'For the first time in years I felt safe'

When you reap the harvest of your land, do not reap to the very edges of your field or gather the gleanings of your harvest. Leave them for the poor and for the foreigner residing among you. I am the LORD your God.

–Leviticus 23.22

Fear of success was one voice I had to battle with (and still do), but there have also always been many other contrary voices swirling around my mind, questioning whether or not I was doing the right thing. When the devil tempted Jesus, he did so by getting him to doubt foundational beliefs about himself and his ministry, suggesting he could use his time better. Satan tries twice with the taunt: '*If* you are the Son of God . . .' and another time with: '*If* you worship me, it will all be yours.'[1]

Even well into running Hope into Action, I would watch overseas crises unfolding, with friends flying out to countries like Lebanon, Syria or the Central African Republic, and think: I really know my way around that line of work better than what I'm doing in the UK. Surely, I would be more help there than I am here. The beneficiaries are in greater need, and I would be helping more people.

Unbeknown to him, Matt from Wolverhampton did something to help me through this maze of misgivings.

As we had developed our work, we had looked into whether we could house asylum seekers and refugees, but had concluded that in Peterborough, unlike some other cities, there weren't many who were destitute and homeless.

Meanwhile, Matt had been having meetings with The Refugee and Migrant Centre in Wolverhampton, which was struggling to house large numbers of homeless refugees. The situation in Wolverhampton was really difficult: authorities were struggling to cope, charities were overwhelmed and housing was insufficient. As always with Matt, he grasped issues superfast, and then his entrepreneurial spirit and rapid mind were already working out solutions.

Having felt that housing refugees was another area of deeper water God was calling us to – another people in need 'on the other side' of our society – it was a wonderful moment when Matt told me we had housed our first refugee in a Hope into Action home.

The needs of refugees were obviously very different from those of many of our tenants at that time, and Matt set about adapting our model to reflect their requirements. He wasn't generally dealing with individuals who had addictions or were tempted towards crime. Many of their practical challenges stemmed rather from their poor or almost non-existent English. They were often of the Muslim faith, and many were highly motivated to work or be educated.

Matt got busy enrolling tenants on English courses and helping them find work. He facilitated interaction with churches, encouraging volunteers to invite tenants for meals and helping them become aware of the issue of halal meat. He adapted both the model and our houses in the light of the tenants' needs and wishes, realizing that while we normally housed two or three people in a home, his tenants often found it culturally appropriate and economically preferable to have four people in a home.

Shortly before a visit to Wolverhampton, I asked Matt if I could meet any of his refugee tenants. He explained that he was just moving someone in from Sudan and asked if I would like to meet him. My arms literally came up in goose bumps. It felt as though the two parts of my world had collided and my dual passions had met. So a few days later, there in Matt's church office, I sat on a couch in a cold reception area with Abdul.

People often say it is unwise to ask too many intrusive questions about someone's background, but when you know and understand where someone has come from, the conversation flows very naturally.

'So which part of Sudan are you from?' I asked.

'Darfur,' Abdul replied.

'Which part of Darfur?'

'West Darfur.'

'Which part of West Darfur?'

'Geneina.'

'I know Geneina. Which part of Geneina?'

'Well, I'm actually from a village not far from there called Beida.'

I could barely hold back my excitement now. 'Beida!' I squeaked. 'I know Beida! I was there from 2005 to 2008. Do you remember Tearfund?'

Abdul looked at me with incredulity, his eyes full of amazement and delight. We both felt that spark of connectedness, of understanding. I knew his home. He knew my past environment.

As we batted our conversation back and forth, exchanging familiar parts of our lives, I discovered Abdul had actually been in one of our camps as a child. He had taken part in some of the health activities groups that Rach had worked on, and he remembered my colleague Annie, a child psychologist.

Abdul shared with me some of the horror of what had happened to him – atrocities that had forced him to leave his beloved homeland and family. He described how the Janjaweed had descended on his village in 2014, killing people, assaulting women, injuring many and burning the buildings to the ground. As he spoke, his dignified composure gave way at times to raw emotion, his voice trembling as he recounted the tragic events he had experienced. From time to time he would choke up and have to pause while he composed himself.

Sadly, Abdul's difficulties did not end in Sudan. He continued his story, describing his challenges as he tried to reach safety – which he also later recorded for us:

The journey to the UK was long, lonely and absolutely terrifying. I left Darfur in August 2014 and fled through Egypt, before crossing the Mediterranean Sea in a small, overcrowded boat full of complete strangers. I didn't know anyone; I was completely alone and scared. Before we took to the sea, we knew that other boats had sunk and people had drowned, but we were so desperate that we got in anyway – it was worth the risk. The boat wasn't safe; it started to take on water and in the end we had to be rescued by a bigger ship, which took us to shore.

We finally reached Italy in September 2014, after 13 days at sea. I then made my way from Italy to a refugee camp in France, where I spent many months. I was physically and emotionally exhausted, but I knew I still had to keep going. After many unsuccessful attempts, I managed to get across to Dover, by hiding underneath a lorry and clinging on to the wheel axle all the way through the Channel Tunnel. I volunteered myself to the police when we reached Dover, and I was taken to an immigration centre, where I stayed for three days, and was then sent to London. From London I went to Birmingham, before finally ending up in Wolverhampton.

When I was eventually granted asylum, after 12 months of living like a prisoner in an immigration centre, I was given 28 days to move out of the government facility. Once again, I was alone and homeless. I sofa-surfed with another asylum seeker for a while, but when his asylum was granted we knew our time had run out again and we would soon have nowhere to go. Thankfully, someone from the refugee centre introduced us to Matt, and we were housed in a home run by Hope into Action.

For the first time in years I felt safe. I had a home; I belonged somewhere – it was an amazing feeling. The frightening things I experienced in my home country and on my journey to this point still linger in my mind, and it scares me to think of what could have turned out differently.

As Abdul shared his experiences with me, I could see he was taking on board afresh the reality of the danger he had faced. I felt in him a realization of his vulnerability, a sense of disbelief that he had really engaged in such danger 'willingly', and a startled recognition of how close he had come to death.

I sat looking at him. So young, yet having already experienced so much. The nameless, faceless term 'refugee' became a real person: a real person with real emotions, real needs, real trauma. Hearing him share his story brought into reality for me the raw pain and fear experienced by those who have to flee their countries. As he shared his story, I realized he had felt everything in exactly the same way as I would have if I'd been in his place.

There is so much media coverage about refugees in this country and others, and the vast majority seems to be negative. Donald Trump used the word 'vermin', and the refugee camp in Calais was nicknamed the 'jungle', with many of its occupants repeatedly referred to as 'migrants' rather than 'refugees'. In radio phone-ins, people would call them 'scroungers' and argue that the UK benefit system was too lenient, and we shouldn't help them when there was already a housing crisis.

Nine years of living and working in conflict areas – meeting and seeing the plight of war-affected communities – had not immunized me against absorbing the opinions expressed around me and in the media (or, in the words of Isaiah 58 again, the opinions expressed with 'the pointing finger and malicious talk'[2]). When I met Abdul and other refugees, though, some of those views that I had unconsciously taken on board dissolved. Slowly, the hard edges around my heart began to melt away, like candle wax, as they experienced the flame of truth and I encountered real people suffering real problems. I think of Ahmed, one of our tenants from Syria, racked by pain in his back after being violently attacked and whipped with a rifle butt, still waking up every night, years after the attack, with the same recurring nightmare. And his eight-year-old daughter, still suffering night terrors and wetting her bed after the horrors she had already experienced as a small child. Such things should not happen to anyone. I came to see we have the privilege of shining the light of Christ's compassion into places where darkness has taken a grip.

There are plenty of areas of our faith that can be discussed and argued about, but I find very little wriggle room, in either the Old or New Testament, on the issue of refugees. 'Do not betray the refugees,' insists Isaiah. 'Hide the fugitives.'[3] 'Do not ill-treat or oppress a foreigner,' instructs the law in Exodus.[4] 'Do not forget to show hospitality to strangers,' writes the author of Hebrews.[5] And if you are still not convinced, take it up with the most famous refugee of all time: Jesus!

Matt has expanded his work to include destitute asylum seekers, taking in people with no recourse to public funds and advocating for them to have justice in this land. From his first pioneering efforts, we now have over ten homes for refugees across England. Our work has included engaging with the Syrian Vulnerable Persons Resettlement Scheme to help churches house Syrians coming directly from refugee camps. We have housed well over a hundred refugees, including those from Sudan, Syria, Kuwait, Iran, Iraq, Afghanistan, Eritrea and the Democratic Republic of Congo. We've housed Muslims. We've housed Christians, including those who have fled terrible persecution for their faith. Sometimes we've successfully housed Muslims and Christians together.

Some of our tenants have been extremely affected by war and are almost certainly suffering with some form of PTSD. However, until they have a home and someone to help them through the system, it is extremely difficult for them to make progress in this country. Rather than seeing them as threats (or as one person once said to me, 'terrorists'), we may do better to see them as a rich resource for our nation. I would also argue we can see their arrival as a tremendous opportunity, including for the Church. The future faith-leaders for the UK are now at the border. God is sending his reinforcements. It's the spiritually astute who see this. We've had a Muslim Iranian come to faith. We've housed a Christian Arabic-speaking refugee who feels his mission in the UK is to share the gospel with Muslims.

We've also had plenty of Muslims who have shown no interest in Christianity at all. However, they will always be able to look back and say that, at a critical time in their transition, the Church was vital in helping them get over trauma and build a life and future for themselves. And that is what we class as success: the Church has loved the vulnerable. We have loved Jesus, disguised as a refugee – maybe with a strange culture, maybe with a strange language – but if we have loved him and cared for his physical and emotional needs, then we have succeeded. We have fulfilled our biblical obligation to 'show hospitality to the stranger'.

While we were seeking to respond to Jesus' mandate to take care of the foreigner in our midst, we were finding equally challenging needs much closer to home.

38

Pamela

Can a mother forget the baby at her breast and have no compassion on the child she has borne?

–Isaiah 49.15

The *Countdown* timer was ticking away on the television in the background as I sat with Pamela in the lounge of her new home. Pamela was short and slim with red hair and a shy disposition. That day she was feeling unwell and was hunched up, seemingly oblivious to the noise in the background. She raised her head slowly, looked up at the screen, and then, in five seconds flat, answered the conundrum and returned to looking drowsy. Meanwhile, the contestants and audience sat stumped by the challenge.

Pamela had come to faith while in prison; she had previously been an alcoholic but had stayed dry on release. We had taken care of her when she was released and provided her with a home.

Pamela later became pregnant, and when her daughter, Gabby, was born, she and the father, Adam, did a good job of caring for her. However, Pamela fell ill with post-partum depression. As there was no family to help, social services stepped in to care for Gabby. During this time Pamela received a call from an assessor who spoke to her over the phone for an hour. It was concluded that Pamela was psychotic. None of those who had been involved with her considered that assessment to be accurate – and this continues to be the case to this day.

After two months Pamela recovered, but by that time, court proceedings for adoption of Gabby were already in progress. We went to numerous meetings, but were left baffled by the confusion of jargon and processes. When Pamela saw the medical report, she was upset to discover it warned that the baby could be suffering from alcohol withdrawal syndrome, even though she had been proven in tests to be dry for two years before the pregnancy, as well as during it. We both felt that the system had turned against her, with various small injustices taking place along the way, and were looking to the court for the chance to tell her side of the story and be truly listened to. We turned up at the hearing – me in my best suit – ready to give testimony, explain the unfair nature of the process Pamela and Adam had been through, and show why they were able to look after Gabby. However, we were shocked to be told that we would be unable to participate in the hearing. Pamela didn't even get the chance to be heard by the judge. After hours of waiting, she and Adam were called inside. Just five minutes later they were back out again, Pamela in fits of tears, her whole body heaving as she sobbed. Five minutes to be told her fate: Gabby had been irreversibly adopted by another family.

Few things have I found harder to process in my ten years with Hope into Action than that court decision.

While I found this situation harrowing, there is, of course, much important work that is done by social services, and their case workers do have to make incredibly difficult decisions. This decision was also far from easy. I was, however, surprised at how hard I found it to understand and follow the process that social services went through, even after attending meetings alongside the parents. If I found it baffling and disempowering, I imagine many mothers do too. I also know I am not alone in thinking the system has become more brutal in recent years. Others with much greater expertise than I possess have also shared this opinion.

As a middle-class Christian, I grew up hearing about adoption (I can actually remember the first time my mum explained it to me). However, I never heard anyone talk about the mothers or families left behind, or the silent grief for removed children that hundreds in this country experience every year. Whether or not the adoption route is 'right' for their child (and of course many times it *is* right), the family left behind will feel a profound loss, coupled with a sense that the state has violated and stolen from them. Those who grew up in the care system are over-represented in prisons, and I do wonder how they weigh the crimes the state punishes them for (which I don't condone) with the perceived 'violations' they feel the state has inflicted upon them.

The cost to the mothers is enormous. Some of them block the pain with drugs, while others find the strength not to. There is very little left for them, not to mention the children's brothers, sisters and fathers. The removal of a child is like a death sentence, yet without the finality, as they never know whether they will be reunited or even see their child again. Our experience is that each one of these mothers loves her children dearly. For a mother to be told by the state authorities that she is not a good parent goes right to the core of who she is. It attacks her sense of worth and robs her of dignity. I am no social worker, and I recognize how hard such work must be. However, experiencing this outcome with the mothers has been painful. It is certainly the area of work I have found the hardest to deal with. At times, all I can do is recognize that Jesus wept, and sometimes that is all we have left. How much more must God feel for, and with, every mother! I sense that those left behind are some of the ones God's heart must pine for the most. He lost his son. The pain was more than we will ever know.

In trying to process this, I have noticed that there are mothers in the Bible who were separated from their sons, including the mothers of Moses and Samuel. Despite the heartache, it wasn't the end of the story. God used their children mightily, and the mothers have been remembered in the Bible and throughout history.

We had another mother, Janine, who came to us with her child when she was homeless. She was an affable, lovely person, bubbly, warm and very hard not to like, with blonde hair and a little bit of sass to her. She did so well as a mother, and I was impressed with how she engaged with her child. I remember her being interviewed by a Radio 1 DJ and being able to articulate her poverty so clearly, explaining, 'Even though I'm only twenty-three, I know how much houses cost, and I simply cannot see how I, as a single mum, will ever be able to buy one.'

Janine always engaged well with the church and us. Then, after she had been with us about a year, we didn't hear from her for a few days. When we found her, she had been beaten black and blue by a former partner (not the father of her child), who had also put a staple into her head. Rightly, social services became concerned for the safety and mental health of the child. A few months later the child was taken away from her. Janine continued to meet this man, who continued to physically abuse her. Within a few months she died of an overdose.

In all these things, we experience highs and lows. Dealing with children being removed and the pain of their mothers is definitely a major low.

However, we also have many, many highs where we are able to help and see positive outcomes for those we engage with. I think of a young woman called Cath who came to our door in Peterborough with nowhere to live. She seemed in a terrible state, and we were moved to help. We found her some food and asked her about her situation. She said she had no money for food because she and her two children had become homeless. Cath explained that she had been put into bed-and-breakfast accommodation, but no one was allowed to stay in the guest house between 8 a.m. and 8 p.m. How do you keep two children warm and fed for 12 hours a day? Being poor can be expensive.

After a while, we moved Cath and her children into one of our homes. About six months later, when things had become easier for her, she sent us a card saying:

Hope into Action took me and my two sons in and gave me a place I could finally call a home. You took me in when I was at my weakest. I have had my ups and downs, but you and the Hope into Action team have made me have more ups than downs. You have pulled me through when I have hit bad times and made me realize a lot, even how to find God. There is so much you have done for me – to you, it's your job, but to me it means a lot more. Words are hard to find to describe it. But I always wonder what if I hadn't had God directing me to you and Hope into Action, how bad things could have got and what I wouldn't have today that I do have. Almost certainly I would have lost my children. I just want you to know how thankful I really am to you, the church mentors and the Hope into Action team. May God bless you all.

39

'The poverty of being unloved is the greatest poverty'

It takes a village to raise a child.

–African proverb

I won't forget meeting a woman I will call Helen. She was well dressed and had a pretty face with a smattering of make-up. She looked quite the part of an office professional and spoke politely while keeping eye contact.

When Helen was initially referred to us by a local agency in Cambridge, I wondered whether we should really be helping her. She seemed so together and had no drink or drug misuse issues. As we knew the person who had referred her, we trusted there must be more going on than met the eye; had we gone on our initial impression, we would have overlooked her and her deep needs that lay within. As we got to know Helen, we realized that life was indeed very challenging for her. At times I would find her crying, and my colleagues told me she was depressed, often in tears and unable to hold down work, tenancies or relationships.

Helen's issues were different from many that we encounter, but were rooted in a very difficult start to life: she had been in care.

We were able to give Helen a home and to help her with some of the challenges she faced. Although she was very private and kept to herself, after she had been with us for about 18 months she asked if she could write something for us. And here it is:

Hello. I am a tenant with Hope into Action. I'm quite a private person and prefer to remain anonymous. I would like to say how blessed I feel to have become friends with Hope into Action and how much I appreciate their help and support. I am very grateful to the local churches and investors for providing a roof over my head. Poverty plays a massive role in the breakdown of our society. Not only does it tie people's hands financially, but also psychologically. My mother was a single parent. Her mother was a single parent with eight children. She had to flee from domestic violence, and life was difficult for her and for my mum and her brothers and sisters. Everything was a struggle, which left everyone feeling hopeless and devoid of love. The little things many people take for granted were difficult, like being able to pay bills and rent and having food every day, as well as feeling part of a loving family or community. My mother suffered with mental illness, depression and low self-esteem. I had to go into foster care, which was extremely difficult for me, and I experienced trauma, violence and terrible things that no child should have to witness or experience. I spent most of my childhood and teenage years feeling disheartened, frightened, lonely, inadequate and hopeless.

We think sometimes that poverty is only being hungry, naked and homeless. The poverty of being unwanted, unloved and uncared for is the greatest poverty.[1]

On leaving care, I became homeless and ended up in a couple of abusive relationships as I was vulnerable and needy. I struggled to make friends and hold down jobs as I had low self-confidence and very little support or guidance. On meeting Hope into Action and receiving their help and support, I have managed to turn my life of misery and abuse around to a more positive and happy one. Hope into Action is integral for our society because it hears the unheard and helps the forgotten. One thing I have noticed from the people who come to Hope into Action for help is that they have tremendous courage. It takes courage to come from a broken family. It takes courage to face constant adversity, and it takes courage to ask for help, because everything is an uphill struggle.

Helen's writing highlights the challenges faced by all too many in this country. In our work we are constantly dealing with the impact that starting life in care has upon a person.

At the time Helen wrote this piece we were housing Carrie, another care leaver. Carrie looked about 12, with an innocent and vulnerable face. She was petite in stature and shy in personality. However, she had been used as a 'lookout' (someone who walks around near a crime scene and looks out for the police) and a 'mule' (someone who carries hidden drugs, often in a bra) in some significant crimes, though she had never been caught. She had lost her child to adoption and was devastated by the separation. She had also lost her grandmother (her 'nan'), who had kept the family together more than anyone, and was still grieving for her. When she came to us she had a partner, but, although he was a likeable character and they loved each other, there were financial and other forms of abuse and the relationship broke down.

When we first met Carrie, we suggested she might like to consider having two befrienders from her supporting church, one of a similar age to her and the other a grandmother figure whose name was Tina. She built a great relationship with both befrienders, and especially enjoyed the times she would sit and knit with Tina, as it reminded her of the times she had spent with her nan.

Tina was a kind woman, who had worshipped in a local church in Peterborough all her life, and she forged a brilliant connection with Carrie.

Just before Christmas, Tina and I were the first to arrive at a prayer meeting, and we got chatting about Carrie.

'I've never met anyone quite like Carrie,' she said. 'The emotional challenges she faces are extraordinary. How she even gets out of bed each morning, I don't know. I admire her so much.'

'You know, Ed,' she continued, 'I never knew people like this actually existed. These people who have left care are the "lost sheep" that Jesus was referring to, aren't they?'[2]

This lovely lady, kind-hearted and so willing to help, had never been exposed to such need throughout her Christian life. It struck me as an interesting indictment of the Church that our lifelong members have had little exposure to the vulnerable in our society, even though they live so near.

Yet care leavers perfectly fit the profile of those to whom we are called to offer love and support. They are over-represented in prostitution, prison and unemployment queues, and among street sleepers and sex-gang victims. Statistics show that 31 per cent of women and 24 per cent of men in the adult prison population come from care, and Home Office figures report that 70 per cent of prostitutes have spent time in care. Other research shows that at the age of 20, 40 per cent of care leavers are not in education, employment or training.[3]

Tina was right. We have to leave those 99 sheep who are already sitting in church, and go to find the one that's missing. We need to go out into the mire, into the bog, on to the craggy cliff edge and hear the voice of the bleating 'lost sheep'. Our mission is to help church members get out into that world in a relational, long-term way and to do so showing respect and humility.

These twin qualities of respect and humility are key. I have been to festivals and heard speakers use the term 'lost, least and last' as a rallying cry to thousands, with many responding to the call to evangelize such people. Each word is a reference from the Bible – I get that – but I leave those experiences wondering if there is something in the 'tone' that is not quite right. In every one of the tenants I have met, I see enormous resolve, ingenuity, talent and gifts, even if they are not always able to see those traits in themselves. They have inspired me time and again with their courage and fortitude. The trouble with calling them '*lost* sheep' or 'the *least* of these' is that it creates a subconscious superiority among 'us' towards 'them'. As Christians, we share in common an understanding of how deeply flawed we are: we have seen into our own hearts and the zoo of lusts and selfishness that exists there. We recognize we are equal to all others and are ourselves in need of being saved. Sometimes our rallying cry to save the 'least' might promote a sense of an inequality of power. 'Take nothing with you on the journey,' was Jesus' first command to his disciples on mission.[4] No clothes, no food, no preconceived ideas. That'll keep you humble.

Carrie has moved on from Peterborough and away from her boyfriend. She is now with another partner and they have a child together. This one they have been able to keep.

And Helen, the woman who wrote the account earlier in this chapter? The other day – five years after we first took her in and a long time after she had moved on – I received a text from her: 'Hi Ed, I got the sales assistant job (smiling emoji face).' That might not sound like much, but, after all she'd been through and all her effort and determination to get off the ground, this was a major success; I could have punched the air with delight.

I was long familiar with the African proverb that it takes a village to raise a child. More recently, I have come to wonder whether it takes a church to raise someone out of relational poverty and homelessness.

40

Rain in the springtime

Ask the LORD for rain in the springtime.

–Zechariah 10.1

Shortly after the prayer meeting with Tina, I had an 'away day' with the trustees to discuss plans for our future growth. By now the Conservatives had won the general election of 2015, and austerity and cuts were biting. However, as an organization we had been expanding geographically and were now operational in ten cities. It occurred to us that if we grew by two homes per city per year, we would increase by 20 new houses a year.

Somewhere between the autumn of that year and the worst of the winter setting in, I had stumbled upon a Bible verse that struck me between the eyes: 'Ask the LORD for rain in the springtime.'[1] It was a text stashed away in the depths of the book of Zechariah, so heaven only knows (literally) how I had come upon it. However, once I had, I couldn't get it out of my mind; it stayed there for a few months, right into Christmastime.

In early January I sat down with our senior managers to reset our objectives – something we do each new year. I confidently proclaimed I would 'Raise 16 new investments by September 2016'. It had a nice ring to it, a bit like our aim of being in 20 towns by 2020 (which happened in 2019, by the way). This was, as all management gurus will note, a specific, measurable, time-bound objective. But was it achievable? The look on my colleagues' faces suggested not only that it was not, but also that I was going half crazy.

A week later at our staff away day I said to everyone, 'I think this is our verse for the year. I'm asking the Lord for rain and am confident he will answer. You go back to your cities and prepare the land [that is, get some churches ready] because I can assure you the rain is coming.'

That night, as I reflected on what I had said, I came to the conclusion that I had, in fact, been a pompous idiot. What had I just said? I don't like the power that comes with those types of comments, as if one somehow has a hotline to God. Who exactly do you think you are, Mr High-and-mighty-Walker?

Well, whatever the rights and wrongs of saying that, I can tell you this: by September 2016 we had raised a further 18 new investments – and I have no idea how. We had planned to run an email campaign, but we didn't need to: the rain just kept falling without any effort on our part. In 2017 we opened more houses than in any other year, increasing our number of properties from 35 to 51.

The rain didn't just land in *my* lap: it was everywhere.

It was falling in Wolverhampton on Matt. At the beginning of the year, he had been about to write an email saying he'd been unable to find matching funds for a grant. He scheduled the task for the next day, but that very night someone whom he barely knew emailed to say he wanted to invest over double the amount needed. Instead of writing to say they'd had no joy, Matt was able to accept the funds and buy another house.

The stories keep coming. Jesus keeps multiplying the bread, and we just try to keep up.

41

'Do you know who I am?'

What good is it for someone to gain the whole world, yet forfeit their soul?

–Jesus in Mark 8.36

'Just seen you on *Look East*. How can I help?'

This was the only message we got through our <info@ hopeintoaction.org.uk> email address after we had been featured on our regional TV news programme.

'How shall I handle this one?' asked Carole, our staff member responsible for receiving these mails.

'It seems a strange thing to write – probably not worth replying to, but best we do just in case,' I replied. 'Can you send him a polite email in response?'

A day or so later Carole came back to me: 'Erm, Ed, I spoke to the man, and this might be one for you. All he said was: "Do you know who I am? I suggest you look me up."'

She had looked him up and had discovered that he was a retired billionaire who had settled in the east of England. He had seen our piece on *Look East* and was keen to meet.

The appointment took a little while to get into the diary as he had just taken his private helicopter to a golf course in Ireland.

On the day of the meeting, my satnav took me to his address, but there was no entrance, only a brick wall. I drove alongside the imposing structure, taking a right turn down a country lane. On and on I went. Finally, I reached a large gate and pulled in as far as I could to use the intercom. The gates opened and I drove up through the gardens, along the winding tarmac road, via a set of ponds and past some conifers, until I finally came to a stop, parking my little car alongside a luxury sedan and two sports vehicles, both neatly covered.

As I squeezed out of the car, I was met by the towering presence of my new billionaire acquaintance. Owen, as I shall call him, greeted me in a warm, avuncular tone wrapped in a thick Welsh accent. He took me into the house through the garage, led me through a pool room with a circular glass ceiling, via a study the size of my lounge, into an even bigger kitchen, and then, eventually, we made it to his sitting room – not far off the size of a tennis court. He went to make a coffee while I disappeared into one of his deep sofas. I struggled to think how I could articulate – even to myself – how amazing the house was; my vocabulary just didn't have enough words about interior decorating. I should have paid more attention to those housing programmes Rach watches. As I sat there, staring at the family photos of him with his children, I wondered what my next line should be. 'Lovely place you have here' didn't seem to fit. I searched all the other conversation cards and starters I had in my repertoire and was left feeling socially inadequate.

Owen returned and passed me my coffee. As I wrestled my way out of the sofa to reach for my cup, I noticed that his gold watch looked heavier than my hammer. I realized I felt more comfortable meeting inmates in prison.

I needn't have worried about small-talk pleasantries. After asking me about what I did, his second question was: 'You can't make a million pounds doing that. How much do you earn?'

I couldn't believe it. Exactly the same question the previous billionaire had asked! At least I now felt on a more secure social footing.

Owen was, as I had researched, a self-made billionaire. In the course of the conversation, he revealed that his sister had been in prison and had died of a heroin overdose. Her three children had been taken into care.

The meeting lasted 20–30 minutes, and I was soon taking the long drive back to Peterborough. As I drove, I worked through the conversation. I remembered reading that some people affected by abuse block the pain with addiction, and others do so by becoming 'super-achievers'; sometimes both can happen in the same family. The piece on *Look East*, which had originally triggered Owen's enquiry, had been about a family in which the mother had been in prison and the kids had been put into care during her stint. She had come to live in one of our homes, had given up drugs and was able to be reunited with her children. I started to wonder if some of these pieces might fit together. When Owen spoke about his sister and her children (as he did two or three times), his voice changed. She had died a couple of decades ago, but the emotion still felt raw.

I remembered the words of Jesus: 'What good is it for someone to gain the whole world, yet forfeit their soul?'[1] A soul overwhelmed with peace is worth more than an account overflowing with wealth. I didn't know whether the verse was relevant to him, but, either way, I resolved to try to pray for him that his soul would be at peace.

He kindly wired us £3,000 a few days later.

42

Palatable good news

Surely, LORD, you bless the righteous; you surround them with your favour as with a shield.

–Psalm 5.12

Over the years we have been privileged to receive a number of awards. We have been honoured to be recognized by various Christian enterprises as well as a number of secular bodies. I am motivated by the thought that something of God's radiant brilliance might reflect in our work and that people of all faiths and none might be struck by it.

We won an award from the Centre for Social Justice (a rightwing think tank) in 2013, another one from the NHS for our work with people in recovery, and various other awards from Christian bodies, such as the Christian Funders Forum.

Heartening though such accolades are, they are never uppermost in our minds. So when Sarah Vassiliades, who now runs our communications and fundraising, mentioned that we might be a candidate for *The Guardian*'s 2017 Public Service Awards, I didn't really pay much attention. The chances of winning seemed low, and I had more than enough spinning plates to keep me busy. When she came back to me a while later to say we'd been invited to an event connected to the awards, I still wasn't paying much attention; it just seemed like one more thing to clog up my mind. As the event got closer and I read the email properly and saw it was in central London and looked a bit upmarket, I thought perhaps it was worth a bit of effort, and I would go to the trouble of putting a tie on.

The invitation allowed Sarah and me to bring two guests with us. On other occasions when we had been invited to award ceremonies, we had taken tenants with us, which had always been a great joy. However, on this occasion, two people were at the forefront of my mind: Richard, who ran our Nottingham operations, and Kate, who ran our Norwich work. Both of them had picked up some bruises and scars along the journey recently. Richard had saved a tenant's life after she had slit her wrists; Kate had been confided in by a tenant and had spent hours with her going through the horrors of her experiences as a victim of sex gangs. They both deserved a bit of a reprieve and a nice night out in London.

As I left the house on the morning of the award ceremony, Rach asked me, 'If you win, will you have to give a speech?'

'Rach,' I replied, 'we are not going to win anything. We're just going for the free food and drink.'

Her question did, however, prompt me to prepare something in my head, just in case.

As we arrived at the grand venue, I started to realize this might actually be quite a big deal in our world. In due course we were called to order for the award ceremony, which was hosted by the actress and comedian Sally Phillips. She made a speech that made us all laugh and was definitely left-wing in angle, with a few lines bashing the then Conservative Government and then some words to praise the work of local councils, all of which sat well with the ethos of *The Guardian*. As she gave out the first awards, which were for other social categories, I realized that virtually everyone else there was representing a town council or a department of a council. *The Guardian* was promoting and encouraging the role of the state. I looked at the names on the shortlist for awards and saw only one other charity mentioned there.

After a while, the presenters moved on to the category for which we had been nominated – *The Guardian* Best Housing Project Award – and played a video in which one of the judges explained why the winner had been selected. Halfway through, I heard him say '. . . and the second reason was the way they have kept their faith as a part of their work'. I knew the result at that moment. It felt surreal to walk forward and receive the award.

I couldn't believe it: we had been selected as the winner from all the organizations involved in housing in England, including councils and housing associations. It was nuts!

The judges were considered intelligent and experienced practitioners in the field, and they saw something special in us. So, just for a moment, we allowed ourselves to celebrate and realize that we are building something unusual, different and special that is bringing honour and glory to God.

We were the only Christian charity there. We were not ashamed of our beliefs, and indeed among the reasons we were noted as standing out from the others were our use of volunteers, who come from the churches, and our faith.

As I travelled home on the train, I thought back to when it was all just a dream in my mind.

I remembered how, when I had returned to the UK in 2008 after three and a half years of living in Khartoum, I had been struck by the thought that it was harder to talk about my faith here in my own country than it was under sharia law. It felt as though the Church was under attack and on the back foot, the state was increasingly pervasive, and the media and society viewed Christians with scorn and derision. In some ways, this philosophy would have been embodied, personified and promoted by *The Guardian* itself. Nine years on, here was *The Guardian* giving us an award and specifically praising us for the impact of our faith.

I was immensely proud that we have put the Church in a central place in our model and somehow made our Christian faith palatable to today's society. I felt honoured that our work can help reveal that our God is alive after all and is good news.

43

The cliff face

It ain't those parts of the Bible that I can't understand that bother me; it's the parts that I do understand.

–*Mark Twain*

From time to time I feel that the pressure of keeping everything together shows on me, and it was at one such moment that Liz, our part-time finance administrator, offered me the opportunity to take a retreat at a small house she owned by the seaside.

I jumped at the chance – Rach gifting me with some time alone – and soon I was in the beautiful Norfolk countryside, drinking in the simultaneous joys of solitude and nature.

On my second day, my interest was waning as I ploughed through a rather hefty tome, and I realized some time outside would be far more uplifting and inspiring. I soon found myself walking along the beach from Sheringham to Cromer. It was February, cold, clear and blustery. To my left was the sea, to my right a high, very steep, grassy cliff. About 400 yards behind me was a path to the top of the cliff, and I decided I would go up it to see the view from the summit before I went back to the house. However, rather than retracing my steps to reach the beginning of the path, it occurred to me it might be a bit of fun to just take the direct route to the top. What a liberating feeling to be free, to have an idea and then, without consultation with anyone else, just go for it! No responsibility for children, no one advising me it was a stupid idea – I was king of my own decisions.

So up I began to climb, with all the unbounded enthusiasm of an eight-year-old boy on his first sprint on to the holiday beach.

The climb was somewhere between the 'challenging' and 'difficult' level, but not something any serious climber couldn't do with his eyes closed. By leaning close to the cliff, getting as much of my feet on to the grass as possible and clinging as tightly as I could to any decent clumps with my hands, I made it to the height of about 30 feet without any problems. No worries.

I then stopped to take in the view. I twisted my body, looked around and admired the North Sea. Then I looked down. I'd done pretty well – maybe 35 feet actually? I looked up. Still about the same distance to go. The cliff looked exactly the same above me as it did below. No reason, therefore, not to be able to make it.

I took another couple of steps up, but this time in a more gingerly fashion, with much reduced gusto. I stopped. Looked up. Then looked down. Fear began to seep into my consciousness.

'Come on, Ed,' I told myself. 'Keep it together. Just crack on and you'll be up in no time.'

No movement.

'Come on. You know you can do it. You've just done half the cliff and not even had a wince of a problem; just get a grip [although to be fair I was already gripping pretty hard] and up you go . . . you muppet.'

My fear grew. No amount of rational thought could shield me from the feeling that this was a very bad place to be and I would be extremely lucky to get down alive. Forget going up: the only question now was whether I could make it down, especially as my legs were wobbling like jelly.

Slowly, step by step, I manoeuvred myself, with virtually my entire body pressed against the cliff, down to the bottom. Once I got to three feet above the sea path, I jumped off, dusted myself down and strutted away, John Wayne style, hoping no one had seen my cowardly, undignified descent or would notice how my jeans were thickly smeared in cliff-face clay. I found the path and trotted up to the top of the cliff, regretting the 20 minutes I had just wasted.

A few weeks later, it occurred to me that midway up the cliff face is how I can feel about Hope into Action. Sometimes I look down at where we have come from and it scares me; I look up at where I think we are going and it scares me still further. All I want to do is jump off the cliff as fast as possible. I lose sleep over issues and have to work hard to ensure my life has balance, variety and exercise, among other things, so that my mind can stay strong and healthy. I tussle with fear, worry about finances, stew on problems, wrestle with insecurity and overanalyse my mistakes. I face an ongoing struggle to calm neurotic thoughts with rational arguments. I am always battling, somewhere deep in the murky recesses of my mind, a suspicion that, despite all our statistical evidence to the contrary, Hope into Action hasn't done anyone any good and is, in fact, just one big con or, worse still, a vanity project. As with the clay on my jeans, I usually hide these thoughts and feelings, except from those very close to me.

I share this, not because I want sympathy, but because I rarely hear other people talk about such things. I have read countless books about heroes, from people of faith to politicians and sports figures. Very few talk about their struggles, worries and insecurities. Perhaps this is even more the case among Christian leaders, who have to battle the dual pride of needing to appear strong while also showing they are trusting in an all-powerful God from whom they draw all the strength they need to cover their weaknesses. I am probably more sensitive than many, and less sensitive than others, but there are days and weeks when my mental health is under pressure. By sharing this here, I hope others who suffer in similar ways may be encouraged, and realize that such struggles are quite normal.

What I know with fair certainty is that I have a relational richness in my life without which my mental health would have suffered far more greatly. Principal among the comfort givers is Rach (I come home and debrief my best and worst thoughts with her every day), then my children, my other family members and my close friends, followed by an outer circle of church and sports mates, all of whom cement me in and hold me tight. I am very aware I am only three missed mortgage payments, a divorce or redundancy away from homelessness or a breakdown. I'd also add that, through it all, the steadfast truth of the nature of God, as revealed in the Psalms and Gospels, is a pillar of strength for me. We long for more of that relational richness and faith to strengthen the homeless up, down and across this country, through the Church.

One source of pressure is the constant struggle to survive financially. Right at the beginning of the journey – even before I knew what we were doing, when I only had the sense that God was calling me to start something – I found myself reading a book called *Nevertheless*, the story of the charity Christians Against Poverty. The people in charge of CAP seemed to lurch from one financial crisis to another with a familiar pattern: they got to the end of the month, they didn't have enough money to pay salaries, staff members agreed to go without salaries for a bit, and eventually God came through for them. I found it terrifying. If I start a book and make it through the first chapter, I will almost always finish it, but I have tried to read this book twice, and both times I could not get to the end. I just couldn't face reading any more of those horrifying tales (which were actually stories of courageous faith followed by miraculous provision). I remember praying, right in the early days, even before I had told anyone anything, 'Lord, if you want me to start a charity, please don't put me through that. I want to be able to pay the staff.'

We were first tested in this when I went full time with only a few thousand pounds in the charity's account and with no major backers and no assurances of any future funding. Month after month, we were able to pay the salaries and still had money left over in the bank. On the one hand I saw every penny that came in, and on the other hand I saw us covering costs that I couldn't quite reconcile with our level of income.

It felt as though Jesus was breaking the loaves, and the loaves were not running out. Every time I looked at the bank statement, we had money to cover the staff costs. Our salary bill is substantial, and every month over the past nine years we have been able to meet our obligations. My early prayer to be able to pay staff was heartfelt. I do believe it has been heard and answered.

It seems our fundraising goes through similar cycles – and each time, my faith wavers.

- *Stage 1.* We do well with a few grants or donations or an event and I begin to relax about money and worry a little less. I start to think we are (or more, I am) getting quite good at this.
- *Stage 2.* Things get a bit tighter and I can see that in a few months' time, unless more money comes in, our reserves are going to dry up. I look around and try to find other sources of income. (Usually this involves mild forms of panic and clutching at many a loose straw, but also some lessons on how to run a charity better.)
- *Stage 3.* Massive sums of money land in our lap from avenues I had no idea even existed. I stop staring at my limited abilities and realize God can take care of our greatest financial needs more easily than I can take care of buying a bag of peanuts. My faith strengthens – briefly.
- *Stage 4.* We start doing well again, and back I go to stage 1. Upstairs, God sighs deeply, looks down on this flawed muppet that he inexplicably loves, and forces me, once again, to abandon pride and fix my eyes on him by plonking me firmly back into the deep end of stage 2.

Occasionally, I am able to stop, take a look at all God has done and wonder in amazement at what has come to pass. I remember how we started this journey during one of the greatest financial crises of the last 50 years. I think of the budget cuts to local government, services and charities, and I consider the number of charities that have folded since we began. When I reflect on all of this, I realize that, if nothing else, the Hope into Action story is one of constant manna landing from heaven, sent by a God able to provide immeasurably more than we can hope or imagine.[1] It is also a story of church after church stepping up, seeing the need, hearing the voice of God, and responding to the call of Christ to go 'to the other side'[2] of society and keep giving.

I hope this account bears testament to that. My fallible faith falters the whole time, like that of anyone else.

Faith, after all, is 'the assurance of things hoped for, the conviction of things not seen'.[3] No more so, in my experience, than when it comes to financial needs. We keep pressing on towards our goals, even while the logical parts of my brain are screaming at me to stop and 'consolidate'. I recall the story of the feeding of the 5,000, and see myself in Philip and the other disciples as they looked with natural eyes at the overwhelming crowd of people needing to be fed. Without faith, I'm not sure how my mind would have coped. However, Jesus seems to keep multiplying the bread, and so we trust he is continuing to direct us.

Financial worries are only one area in which my mental health can struggle. As I look back (or down the cliff face), I remember many challenging situations with our tenants: deaths, evictions, hurts, abuse, sex addictions and affairs, self-harm, suicide attempts, overdoses and recidivism, to name just a few.

Then I look up and realize we will meet more pain. Perhaps the hardest thing of all is when staff or volunteers get hurt. This can foster in me an acute sense of guilt: 'If it wasn't for my bright idea, that wouldn't have happened, and that person wouldn't be suffering right now.' I feel keenly the need to care well for our carers, and we try to ensure this by having strong policies in place.

Yet I am also reminded that this is the space we are called into. Following Jesus, it strikes me, is traumatic. In Luke 8 we read how the disciples got into a boat with him to cross Lake Galilee and were terrified by a sudden storm; when they reached dry land, they encountered a violent and aggressive man, whom Jesus healed; then they watched the extraordinary spectacle of 2,000 pigs rushing down the steep bank to their deaths: more shock, trauma and mess. Jesus led them through all of that for the sake of one homeless man![4] We can therefore conclude that Jesus will lead us into storms and trauma. He calls us, repeatedly, 'to the other side'. This is not a blasé comment. I repeat: we need to look after ourselves and our staff well. However, getting to heaven without bruises might risk the following comment from a battered and bruised angel: 'What? No scars? Was there nothing down there worth fighting for?'

Although much of the work seems hard, that is often because our minds spend more time chewing on the negative than celebrating the positive. Every year we run our stats, and every year we come out with the same results: roughly 90 per cent of the people we have housed maintain their tenancy; roughly 90 per cent of those who have been inside stay out; over 80 per cent of those with drug misuse are improving; nearly 50 per cent have built stronger relationships with their families; nearly 20 per cent are attending church regularly. We are a truly holistic organization.

We are building the kingdom. The crowds are being fed, the homeless are living sustainably, family relationships are strengthening, former addicts are staying clean, former prisoners are staying out of trouble, the vulnerable are finding love, church members are out of their pews, healing is occurring, churches are sharing their wealth with the poor, faith is rising, the kingdom of God is advancing.

44

A week in the life

Seek first his kingdom and his righteousness, and all these things will be given to you as well.

–Jesus in Matthew 6.33

By the summer of 2018 we had over 50 church partners, 55 homes open, and 160 tenants, the vast majority of whom I did not know. As the organization had developed, my role had been adapting, and I was spending less and less time going into prisons and meeting tenants.

On one particular Friday in July, I woke up wondering whether my passion was still running high or whether I was now just a manager.

That afternoon I travelled to a megachurch outside Peterborough for a meeting. I had been building a relationship with the leaders for a few years, and the church had a house with us. I met up with Charles, the Social Action Coordinator, whom I had known for some time and always found to be a kind and lovely man. He introduced me to their finance director, Simon, who struck me as a warm and friendly guy. We began a great meeting, discussing our partnership and a few other issues. I was inspired by all they were doing and the sheer number of lives they were touching. Our house was going well, supporting two young women who had fled domestic violence. I was so impressed by the love being shown to these two ladies. They were both participating in a course run by the church that worked on past hurts. I heard how they were engaging well, and there was a sense of inner and spiritual healing.

Simon was encouraging in his manner and had an evident compassion for the poor. He began asking me about our investment model and how we had got so many houses. I mentioned the parable Jesus told about a rich man storing his grain in barns and then getting more grain and having to build more barns. Jesus concluded the man was a fool.[1]

I said that in our culture we have mountains of Christian wealth in 'barns': our first barn may be a current account; the second, a savings account; the third, an ISA account; the fourth, a pension fund; the fifth, stocks and shares; the sixth – if we are 'doing really well' – a second home, and so on.

Heads were nodding.

I continued, 'In putting our money in these "barns", we are sharing our money with the rich. I recognize we all need banks, but why not also share our money with the poor by investing in a house?'

They were still with me.

'Imagine how much Christian wealth is stored up in barns across this country.'

'Millions,' Simon replied.

I don't usually take the next step, but on this occasion I did: 'I've not looked into your reserves as a church, but I'm sure you have enough in there to buy one house and still have plenty left over.'

I think this probably went too close to the bone.

I waited for Simon's reaction and prepared to back down. I've learned, since my early days, to play the long game, to recognize that the bigger the organization is, the slower the decision-making process will be, and to respect the importance of the consultation that almost all churches engage in. I also know that dipping into hard-earned reserves does not come high on people's agendas.

'Yes, I take your point,' Simon replied graciously, 'but the Charity Commission say we have to have at least six months' reserves and so we need all of that money.'

I'd heard this line before a number of times. I'd looked into it and knew it wasn't true.

'No, actually,' I countered, 'the Charity Commission states that each charity must have a reserves policy. It is up to each organization to decide and be able to justify how much. It doesn't state how many months should be in the reserves, nor that you have to keep them all in the bank.'

Simon, still patient, countered with arguments depressingly familiar.

I just about managed to stay shtum, but inside I could feel my passion rising as I thought: in reality, you have over a thousand people giving you direct debits every month. What are the chances of them all stopping in one month? That risk is, I agree, a theoretical possibility, but how bad does the sermon on Sunday have to be for everyone to stop giving you money the next Monday? Do you really need that much money? Even if you kept the policy at six months in reserves, you could change the policy for some of your reserves to be held in a house, shared with the poor rather than the rich. That way you are not burying your 'talents' so deep.[2]

Thankfully, Charles could sense the tension and wisely managed to steer the conversation on to another topic before it got too heated.

I thanked him at the end for doing so.

While I realized I had probably lost my calm, I was comforted to discover that the passion within still burned bright. By this stage we had been talking for eight years about churches using their reserves to buy homes for the poor, and we had over 50 homes proving that our model worked. We were also in the midst of a rising national homelessness crisis – evident to anyone who went shopping in town. Yet I couldn't think of one church that had been so moved by the poor that it had invested money from its reserves into a house for them. (The vast majority of our investors are individuals or couples.) I caught a glimpse into my subconscious and found evidence that I still cared and could still get upset. I was not just doing a job.

In August that summer, while on holiday, I read these words from Shane Claiborne: 'Redistribution is a description of what happens when people fall in love with each other across class lines.'[3] I reasoned that I needed to get better at introducing finance directors to the poor in a way that makes them fall in love.

What would happen, I thought, if we drew our inspiration from the early disciples? I recalled the well-known passage in Acts 4:

All the believers were one in heart and mind. No one claimed that any of their possessions was their own, but they shared everything they had. With great power the apostles continued to testify to the resurrection of the Lord Jesus. And God's grace was so powerfully at work in them all that there was no needy person among them. For from time to time those who owned land or houses sold them, brought the money from the sales and put it at the apostles' feet, and it was distributed to anyone who had need.[4]

Two days after our meeting, on the following Sunday, I was travelling to Bedfordshire to speak at a church.

I have spoken about Hope into Action at many churches, but I still always prepare each talk individually. While there is so much I could say, getting it across in 20 minutes is a challenge, so I think hard about which aspects to emphasize, praying that God will guide me. I always try to tell at least one story of a tenant, and always pick a recent one. This way my talks are fresh – and if they are fresh to me, then they will hopefully be fresh to those who are listening.

I also try to keep it real, explaining that much of our work is dealing with disappointment. (However, I've learned not to tell the worst. I once gave a talk the week after a heroin addict had relapsed, gone on a binge and sold one of our fridges to get another score. I never heard from that church again. You're the first to hear that story since.)

During the drive up, I tried to listen to what God might be asking me to say. I put on worship music, arrived early and pulled up in a side street. I got out my notebook and scribbled some notes that captured some of my thoughts. Principal among them were the words of Jesus: 'Do not judge.'[5] I was to talk on Jesus meeting the demon-possessed, homeless man from the Gerasenes,[6] a man who had been self-harming, was a prolific and violent offender, was ostracized by the community and had nowhere to sleep. Jesus saw right through all those conditions and saw right into his humanity. He did not judge him by his outer appearance or words. He commanded his followers to do likewise in the Sermon on the Mount.

Pleased with my thoughts, I walked into the church and waited around, chatting to people until the service began. As I sat down I found myself thinking: another middle-class church full of people who don't really know about the real world.

When I was invited up to speak, I shared the thoughts I had jotted down, and emphasized how Jesus valued this rejected, unloved man far more than vital community assets worth hundreds of thousands of pounds (the 2,000 pigs). His love for this despised man was so great that he wrote the pigs off in the blink of an eye in order to save him. It is an incredible story of a God who loves those whom we find unlovable.

At the end of the talk, the minister led everyone in a time of response, and it was touching to hear people stand up and share how they had been moved.

When the service was over, I stayed around and spoke to a few people. One lady, who struck me as properly middle class, revealed that she had been inside and served time. Another person told me he had been homeless here in the town and wished he had received exactly the kind of help offered by Hope into Action. He had now come off drink and was a member of the church community. Then an elderly woman came over to talk and, within minutes, became quite emotional. She told me how her son was living with addiction and was sleeping rough in France. She had recently been out to visit him for a week. She recounted how she would go off to her hotel room and leave him on the streets every night. Chained to his love of and need for heroin, he seemed to prefer French alleyways to a bed.

'What should I do?' she asked, her watery eyes pleading for a magic bullet.

Of course, I could give her no easy answer: there isn't one. All I could do was listen some more and then pray with her.

Before I left, the minister appeared through a bustling throng of people and intoned enthusiastically, 'You should meet our treasurer.'

After my experience earlier in the week, I was not too keen. As my brain hunted frantically for a plausible excuse, I found my lips parting into an insincere smile as the words came out: 'That would be lovely.'

The treasurer turned out to be a delight. 'I love what you're doing,' she said, her bubbly personality awash with enthusiasm. 'If we can get a multiple-investor house going, I'd love the church to put in the first ten thousand pounds from its reserves.'

I nearly fell over. I'd never had a conversation like this with a church treasurer. I was so unprepared that I didn't quite know how to answer.

As I drove home feeling elated, I reflected that one never knows what is going on behind people's Christian masks. I reminded myself not to be quick in judging a church – especially when preaching on the subject! I also thought about this remarkable church treasurer and how she was unlike any others I had met in her willingness to use reserves. I also reflected that she was the first treasurer I had met who was neither male nor white.

Two days later, on the Tuesday, I rushed home early from work. Once back, I wished I could stay home with the family, especially as there was also the allure of a World Cup match on TV. However, duty called, and out I must go.

An hour and a quarter later, I arrived at a hotel in Hinckley for the first ever awards ceremony hosted by Homeless Link, a well-respected, national homeless charity that formulates policy and best practice. I met up with Adele, an effervescent lady from Coventry who had just begun a franchise. She shared about how well the new house was going, and how she could already see change in the tenants. We were still getting caught up as they called us in for the ceremony. The room was packed, heaving with professionals and representatives from lots of large organizations. Not too surprising, as there were 150 organizations being considered for the six awards, with some of the most experienced professionals in the country judging.

The category that we had been nominated for, 'Excellence in Innovation in Housing', was third up, with three organizations shortlisted.

We won't win this, I thought to myself as they announced the nominees.

'And the winner is . . .'

'. . . Hope into Action.'

I couldn't believe it.

Amazed, I made my way through a mass of tables to collect the award – with Adele right behind me – and heard the words over the speaker: 'They work with churches to sustainably and holistically house the homeless.'

On the way home, I thought through the evening and the significance of what had happened.

Although we don't pursue such recognition, the award was nevertheless a tremendous endorsement. In a cynical and increasingly secular world, I was proud to be associated with churches being awarded for doing a good job.

I reflected on what really makes us innovative and unique. We don't set targets around the number of houses we open (we have never even done a marketing campaign to raise more investments). Nor do we have key performance indicators around 'outcomes', 'transforming lives' or 'helping people'.

Rather, our innovation, I reasoned, is that at the heart of our vision is the word 'love'. It is also that we define success as a situation where members of churches are 'out of their pews' and there is an exchange of love with our 'tenants' (not clients).

The use of the word 'love' makes us fairly unique in the homeless sector. It is from focusing on, trying to understand and celebrating love that we get these wonderful outcomes; it is also the reason why others somehow come to the conclusion we are worth an award.

How much of a buzz did the award give me? Well, some, I'll admit. But I get just as excited about church volunteers loving their tenants as I get about the award. I suspect God does too. Even though we are proud that 90 per cent of our ex-offenders have not gone back to jail, just that week we visited one of them who had – and we also celebrate that visit as a success.

As I pulled off the A1 into Peterborough, I was struck by the words of Jesus: 'Seek first his kingdom and his righteousness, and all these things will be given to you as well.'[7] If 'God is love',[8] then the kingdom of God must be love. If we seek to build his kingdom through extending love, other things will follow, whether they be outcomes, awards or swanky three-course dinners to receive awards.

I got home to discover England had won a World Cup game on penalties. Miracles cannot stop happening.

The next day, I woke early and wrote a report on the evening for our staff, concluding with the words: 'Our "innovative award-winning" approach, then, is to follow the ancient words of Jesus. Here's to loving with our heart, soul, strength and mind.'

45

Welcoming community

> What if a fragile world is more attracted to God's vision of
> interdependence and sacrificial sharing than to the mirage of
> independence and materialism?
>
> –*Shane Claiborne,* The Irresistible Revolution, *2007*

How then do we 'innovatively' follow those ancient words of Jesus
about loving with heart, soul, strength and mind?[1]

If we are followers of Jesus, we want to understand, as accurately
as we can, the way he did things and then to translate that into the
context in which we work.

Luke tells us that just prior to feeding the 5,000, Jesus welcomed
the crowds, spoke about the kingdom of God and healed those
who needed healing. We can seek to follow his model, learning
how to welcome people, share truth with them and see them
healed.

How do we welcome people into our homes? How do we bring
healing to those who need healing? And what does 'healing' mean
in the context of giving the homeless a home?

From the outset, I have always held and implemented the principle that our homes are to be for all people, just as Christ died for
all. We do not assess or select people based on their belief system.
We are faith based and not faith biased because I have not yet found
a Bible verse that says Jesus healed only those who had a certain
ethnicity, religious persuasion or sexual orientation. His compassion was for the entire crowd – men, women and children. Likewise,
the apostles gave to others according to the criterion of necessity,
distributing resources to 'anyone who had need'.[2] In the same way,

we provide our homes according to need, not creed. We want our homes to welcome every kind of person. Absolutely. And never will that change.

Jesus died for every single individual: refugees from across the world who arrive in the UK, victims of crime, sufferers of abuse, overcomers from trafficking situations – and also perpetrators of crime and abuse.

We believe that Christ not only died for them all, but that he also wants them to have life in all the fullness and abundance that he can give here on earth.

We seek to represent this, among other ways, by always providing high-quality housing. We are blessed that this is borne out through Noel's passion and insistence that the homes are always completed to a top-notch standard.

When we move people in, we want them to be struck by the welcome they receive as they enter the house. I have seen grown men cry as they walk into their new home and see the quality of the workmanship and finish we give the houses. We prioritize giving the church volunteers time to add small acts of kindness that send the message that the person is being received in love.

I have always wanted to give more than 'a room' or 'a hostel bed'. As one tenant who had come from living in hostels said to me: 'In my previous place, I had vomit staining the side of my bedroom wall. You painted my room for me. It made a massive difference. It showed me you cared.'

In one of the first homes we opened, I had stayed up until the small hours finishing the decorating and painting. The church members had gone shopping and had put food in the fridge and cupboards. Months later, one of the tenants stood up in a church and described how he had opened the cupboards and been overwhelmed that people would go to such lengths for him. He felt someone just out of prison didn't deserve that. He went on to say that even after he had moved on, he still kept a can of baked beans to remind him of the generosity of the church. Small acts of kindness can make a big impact.

As well as showing love through providing a quality home, we try to exhibit a non-judgmental heart. That may sound nice and it may sound easy, but the truth is we all, myself certainly included, carry prejudices. Our country is full of bias, and, whether we realize it or not, we absorb it. We only have to look at the language we all understand in our culture: 'benefit cheats', 'scroungers', 'free-loaders', 'migrants from the jungle' (rather than refugees fleeing violence and war), 'chavs', 'smackheads'. There are many more such labels and terms, and they rub off on our attitudes. Essentially, those phrases and the sentiments behind them are the 'malicious talk' that Isaiah 58 denounces. God promises in that chapter that when we do away with the malicious talk, he will answer our prayers and do a load of other cool stuff too, including being our rear guard . . . nice to know he even has my backside covered!

We give regardless of merit. We've shown love to people who have committed crimes; we've shown love to convicted abusers; we've shown love to people who have stolen from their parents or neglected their children. I can guarantee that every single person we have ever housed has been a sinner. We try not to judge or point the finger.

We try to select people who, we believe, are at the point where they want to change, grow and develop. Happily, our record points to the fact that this usually works. However, it hasn't been a fairy tale every single time. Those whom we've helped haven't always thanked us. Sometimes they have taken us for a ride or thrown our efforts back in our face. That can hurt. At times they abuse us, and we have to allow ourselves to be exposed to that. Some days we manage with more grace than others.

While we certainly get wiser as we grow, we try to maintain the fresh heart of God's grace: 'he is kind to the ungrateful and wicked. Be merciful, just as your Father is merciful.'[3] As I spend time thinking about those radical instructions from Jesus, I soon realize I am among the wicked and ungrateful, and I see God's grace to me more clearly. Who, then, am I to withhold grace or kindness from another when it has been so generously poured out to me? Jesus continues:

> Do not judge, and you will not be judged. Do not condemn, and you will not be condemned. Forgive, and you will be forgiven. Give, and it will be given to you. A good measure, pressed down, shaken together and running over, will be poured into your lap.[4]

Easy to understand; hard to put into practice.

Of course, God has given us intelligence and asks us to love him with all our mind. We try to use the best techniques, thinking and approaches that we can come up with or that others have developed. Action plans, monitoring forms and support techniques all form part of our 'welcome' and part of how we hope healing occurs.

As well as adopting a professional approach, we also love to prepare the house by praying over it. At first we did this before the tenants arrived. However, this changed when Bishop Donald of Peterborough came to pray over our tenth home. He led 20 of us, including the new tenants, on a wonderfully earnest prayer walk around the house.

I wasn't quite sure what our three new tenants would make of it all, so when I stayed afterwards to clear up, I asked them, 'So tell me honestly, how was that for you? Sorry if it was a bit awkward with all these Christians.'

They seemed surprised by my question. 'No, it's just so nice to see so many people caring for us,' one of them replied emphatically, as the others nodded. 'You know, our own parents rejected us. We've not had this sort of love before. To see that many people here to care for us was really special.'

Aside from being vital, our house prayers can be moving times that leave all those present, including the tenants, in tears. They come in all sorts of shapes and sizes, reflecting the different spiritualities of our partner churches. I've been moved to tears by prayer times using the Anglican liturgy, and been lifted in my spirit by others in which visions, tongues and prophecies have been shared.

We engage with prayer in whatever form we can find it, including, in these more modern times, via email or text. The impact can clearly be felt, as this message I received in the summer of 2018 from Nigel in mid Sussex shows:

> One of our tenants who came to faith shortly before leaving custody has been struggling recently. He relapsed into drug and alcohol misuse, his mental health has deteriorated, he has begun self-harming and has become increasingly volatile. I met him two weeks ago and told him that I would get our prayer team mobilized. So I sent out a group text message to ask for prayer.
>
> He texted me ten days later: 'I just want you to find those that have been praying for me as it has obviously worked. I have not touched anything now for near enough two weeks, and I don't even feel like I want to touch it, not even been in my head. I've also given up smoking for a week, and I haven't been drinking at all apart from one glass of wine and one fruit cider! So something has worked.'

We seek through all these elements – a good-quality house, thoughtful preparation of the home by the church, a non-judgmental welcome, and prayer – to contribute to the whole healing process. We absolutely believe that Jesus healed in the first century and that he also gives us authority to bring his healing today. It is notable that in most of the Gospel accounts of healings there is an element of concealed alienation that is also in need of healing. The process of full restoration is bound up with over-coming exclusion. If we follow the account of Mark, we meet, early on, a man suffering with leprosy, a sickness profoundly bound up with exclusion. Jesus roots his healing in instructing the man to go and show himself to the priest to rejoin community life. Next Mark introduces us to a paralytic man who, after being physically healed, is instructed by Jesus to go 'home'. Then Mark takes us to a 'demon-possessed' man whom Jesus delivers. Alongside the deliverance, Jesus recognizes his lack of rootedness and commands him to embed himself into his own people[5] and home.[6] Mark then tells us of the bleeding woman, whom Jesus not only heals but also connects to and affirms relationally as his 'daughter'. And so the theme continues, linking from God's words in creation, 'It is not good that man should be alone',[7] to Jesus' repeated practical recognition of the need for connectivity and family. We see it when he heals Peter's mother-in-law, when he directs a widow's son to his mother and, finally, on the cross when he asks John (who is representative of the Church) to care for his own mother, Mary (representative of those in a vulnerable situation). Where imme-diate family isn't available, he redefines family as the Church. We have a fundamental need for relationships. We feel whole when we are connected.

In the words of Rowan Williams:

Somewhere in the background is a brokenness, an emptiness, that needs to be addressed, and into which Jesus speaks; and the act of healing frees the person to express what they are made and called to be, which is members of a community that lives in gratitude and praise . . .[8]

Jesus' healings were, of course, also physical healings. People physi-cally got better. We therefore must pray for and expect physical and emotional healings in our midst.

I remember seeing this at play in a special way when a 22-year-old homeless woman called Sandra was referred to us. She arrived at our offices with her child, who was almost exactly the same age as my daughter Elana. Sandra had an incredible ability to manage her daughter as she talked to us. I was streets behind in my parenting skills. As Sandra spoke, she shared with us that she had a further three children. However, they had been removed by social services, as her partner, the father of her children, had been violent and sexually abusive.

We moved Sandra into one of our homes and she settled in well, and I saw her slowly beginning to grow in confidence. About nine months later, she was at a church-run Bible study and shared what had happened while she had been pregnant with her fourth child. She told the group that social workers had said to her they could not leave the new baby with her and her partner: either she must leave him and move to a new city, or they would have to take the child from her. That night she lay in bed, unable to sleep and with her child kicking within her, and cried out in a form of prayer. She didn't even know what or whom she was crying out to. She certainly didn't know the first thing about God and had never read the Bible or learned about Christianity. However, that night, after crying out, she felt as though she had the strength of an army of 10,000 – 'almost like ten thousand angels were helping me,' she said. The next day she made the decision to leave her partner. Shortly after the birth, she and her baby were moved to Peterborough.

After Sandra told her story to the church group, one of the members shared with her some verses from Psalm 91: 'If you say, "The LORD is my refuge," . . . he will command his angels concerning you to guard you . . ."[9]

Sandra felt the urge to pray further to Jesus. That night she had a dream in which she was having a picnic in a park with all four of her children, and they said to her, 'It's okay, Mum. We're safe. We understand why it happened and we love you.'

She awoke the next morning with an incredible peace – one she hadn't experienced before. She came into the office and, over a coffee, explained to me how she now felt different. 'I now have a sense that they're okay and that one day we will all be united again. I feel so much better about things.'

We had welcomed her into a home; Jesus had done some vital healing.

Sandra's story is just one of many that strengthen our belief in miracles and in a God who can move mountains.

We also believe that another element to healing is faith.

Sometimes we feel it appropriate to encourage tenants to work on spiritual issues that arise. I know we are now straying into a controversial area, and different people reading this will have varying opinions. So let me start off by saying we are against forcing someone into saying a certain type of prayer or taking on any belief system against his or her will. We also understand the power dynamic in some of those situations. We are keen to avoid any hint of spiritual abuse.

We do, however, celebrate 'conversion moments', though we are mindful not to get too triumphant. Experience has taught us that supporting spiritual growth in our tenants takes time. When someone 'becomes a Christian', it neither immediately wipes away a difficult life situation nor instantly changes that individual's character. Even the evangelist Jackie Pullinger in Hong Kong, who has seen amazing spiritual miracles over a long period of time, emphasizes the need for long-term investment:

I have begged people [overseas volunteers] to love the people and stay. The disadvantage of short term is a wrong perspective based on this generation's need for instant results . . . Sometimes everything goes well . . . At other times nothing goes right even here. The man who prophesied last night beats up a helper the next morning, or the whole house runs away. Then the visitor leaves disillusioned . . . The remarkable fact that after so long we still see most addicts who come to us believe in Jesus, pray in tongues and detoxify from drugs painlessly does not obscure the fact that they need a changed mind.[10]

With that preface, can I say we also recognize, unequivocally, that spiritual change can have enormous power to help bring life, wholeness, forgiveness and transcendence to people and to their situations. We can tell stories of men and women who have felt physically and spiritually better, and so 'salvation', our eternal and earthly healing, is a massive cause for celebration.

Some reading this will think that 'conversions' are not right. Well, if we believe in free choice, then let people choose. All I can say is: I know how important my faith is to me here on earth. It has brought me untold guidance, strength and a sense of direction. I can't fully work out how, but my admiration and love for this guy Jesus and his words keeps getting deeper. Why would I not want to talk about and share that? It is the same with everything in life: we talk about what we are enthused by. When my bad back got better, I wanted to let others with the same problem know and help them find a solution. Why would I do anything different with my faith?

If individuals do come to a point where they would claim to have faith, and that faith gives them life, hope, strength, morality and joy, how can that be a bad thing for them or for society? Let's look at what happens when a person starts going to church. Sociologically, any reasoning mind will agree it is good to meet up with others once a week. Psychologically, any reasoning mind will accept that singing is good for the spirit, and the stillness of prayer is good for the mind. Listening for 20 minutes a week to a sermon telling people to love their neighbour can't be bad either.

But why not give the final word to our tenants:

I had gone from enviously successful to a pitiful, homeless, jobless, penniless failure, through a series of breakdowns over a relatively short period of time. I lost everything, my mind was broken, my soul had died, I had lost any spirit I had, and my body was just an empty vessel that I despised.

Well, he gave me faith; he healed me – several times – physically, mentally, emotionally and spiritually. My soul is alive and happy, my spirit is dancing. My mind is centred; depression and the like are a long-gone memory. My voice is coming back. I am blessed, mightily blessed. The change in me is profound.

He gave me faith.

He gave me strength.

He gave me hope.

Anthony, who wrote this, came to us in a very difficult state, depressed and struggling with addiction to a range of drugs. He was a scientist, a statistician and a student of philosophy. He had studied Eastern philosophy, Buddhism, Taoism and Zen. However, he remained unsatisfied: 'There was still something missing in my life and I didn't know what it was.' Then his world came crashing down. At that point he connected with Hope into Action, and in that dark hour of his life we offered him a tenancy. He was invited to church by one of our befrienders, a man called Stuart. This was the turning point. Anthony's long journey of discovery and seeking for truth led him to read the Bible, and everything suddenly fell into place for him. All the aspects of philosophy that he had loved now began to make sense. Jesus was the missing key in the whole picture. He found love in the Bible, God's love: God loved him, and he loved God.

Anthony was befriended by a woman from the church called Flis, who oozed compassion, warmth and empathy to everyone she met. She took Anthony under her wing from the time he moved in, and was deeply attached to him. She shared the following:

I first met Anthony quite soon after he became a Christian. Although quiet and unassuming, Anthony had a brilliant mind and a fiery passion for God's word. In one year, he had read the Bible through three times. He started an online blog and in a very short space of time gathered over a thousand followers, including some pastors. He was an extremely eloquent and beautiful writer. On a personal note, Anthony became a dear friend and brother: a man of great faith, great courage, and a beautiful mind and heart.

Sadly, and for some reason none of us will understand, Anthony became ill with cancer and died shortly afterwards in hospital. In his final hours he was surrounded by people who had been part of his befriender group. Whatever the reasons for his death, no one can deny that the church was something special for him. It had brought him joy and peace in his closing chapter. In all my years of thinking and reading about what makes people change, I haven't come across anything that creates as profound or sustainable a change as finding hope and inner healing through faith in God.

This is why one of the core areas of leadership for me, and for the trustees, is to ensure that the Church remains integral to all we do and that we never lose the centrality of our spirituality.

If I am honest, my dream and one of my deepest prayers is for more miracles and a move of the Holy Spirit to spread among our church partners and our tenants. I often try to step out of myself to look at and rationalize my faith. It puzzles me. Why it is such a driving force within me, I really don't understand. But I do relate to the verses that say if nothing else will declare God's praise, 'the stones will cry out'.[11] From somewhere deep within comes an urge to express my faith[1] and to see others find even a fraction of the strength and life and hope I have from it. I simply cannot shut it up. I am no great evangelist, but I can work hard to create an environment where people are more likely to encounter faith, and I left a job in order to see this happen. That decision has been at the cost of tens of thousands of pounds for me and my family.[12] Not for one moment do I regret it.

Some people count conversions. We do not; how can we really know where someone is spiritually? We do, however, love to celebrate the process of transformation. If I told you every good story that has come out of Hope into Action already, I could write a book five or even 25 times the length of this one. But no one would ever finish it!

46

Sitting on a gold mine

How many loaves do you have?

–Jesus in Mark 6.38

Another intrinsic part of our approach, which perhaps contributes to our innovative model, is that we very much seek to recognize and work with the strengths of those we help.

In many ways, certainly in the early days of Hope into Action, I would often feel out of my depth. I knew a bit about other models of housing that were out there, and I knew ours had to be an improvement. However, I didn't have years of front-line experience in the sector to draw on to give me confidence in what I was doing. As a result, I would often turn back to my memories of working in Africa and draw on principles I had learned there.

I particularly remember my first visit to a remote village in Garsilla in West Darfur. We had flown into a city called Nyala, the dusty capital inhabited by half a million South Darfurians. The chief mode of transport was donkey and cart, and the sand kicked up by the donkeys' hooves created a permanent haze. In no time the sand infiltrated my clothes, nose and hair, and found its way inside my ears, into the folds of my skin, under my nails and into every available pore.

After one night in Nyala, Rach and I departed on the 13-hour drive to get to Garsilla. It was one of the most uncomfortable, hot journeys I had ever taken. The constant bumpy roads made me feel travel sick, so I ate nothing but a few stale chunks of bread the whole day. This, combined with the heat and sickness, meant I also felt tired and weak. Every few hours we would stop the vehicle and get out for some more very hot air, and stretch our legs as our drivers took a break. To be respectful of the local culture, Rach was wearing a *shalwar kameez* headscarf (which covers the hair and some of the face). I would have loved to have held her hand or given her a hug, but that would have been inappropriate; so, on these mini-breaks, while trying not to puke, I was gentleman enough to keep my distance. My fragile health contrasted with hers. We had only been married for seven months, and I could see my young bride had the constitution of an ox. Every now and then, I would sneak a glance at what I could see of her beautiful face, stunningly framed by her turquoise headscarf, and draw strength. Proud of my choice, I spent the 13 hours composing a couple of poems for her.

The next day was our first Valentine's Day as a married couple. We awoke under separate mosquito nets in a mud hut that doubled as the team office. I handed her my poems, and you can imagine her delight when she saw herself likened, in the same verse, to both a fox and an ox.

Our romantic interlude was interrupted by the team outing. We travelled still further and joined in a workshop with local men and women who were leaders in their community. They shared their experiences of war, displacement, brutal violence, theft of their cattle and land, burning of their villages and polluting of their water points. They went on to give a long list of all their needs, from medical care to seeds, to education, to treatment for malnutrition. It was a depressing series of tales of woe and lack. After lunch we came back and took them through an exercise of analysing all that they had. On the surface, they had lost everything. But as the questions were asked in different ways, they began to see their strengths and resources, or 'assets' as we called them: strong community, excellent knowledge of the land, vast open spaces to regrow their herds, available labour, many teachers and nurses who had fled into the camps, arable farmers who understood local crops, nearby trees that could provide wood for construction or sale, and so on. Soon we came to see there were a great many resources that we could build on; our woe turned to hope and resolve. Good development, even in the fiery aftermath of a disaster, can and should be built on the capacities of the people. Now the relationship and conversation changed from 'You need to give us loads of stuff for our needs' to 'We can do this ourselves . . . we would like your support in some, but not all, areas'.

In many ways, all good poverty alleviation is built upon this same approach. It is so easy to see what is lacking – to be aware of our needs. It is the same whether one is doing community development in a rural African village, counselling a deeply abused or hurt adult, or working with someone on the streets. However, I would argue (as would many professionals) that helping is done best when building on the resources of those one is seeking to support. Jesus used the same approach. In the feeding of the 5,000, his disciples were faced with an overwhelming problem and felt inadequate for the task. Into this situation Jesus asked, 'How many loaves do you have?'

Doing the above exercises all over Darfur and other parts of Africa changed my perspective. Where once I had arrived in a village and been struck by the incredible poverty (skinny, pot-bellied children; mud huts; limited facilities), now I would see enormous potential wherever I went. So too with the homeless: they have enormous strengths, ingenuity, energy, talents and insights. Part of our role is to help them see and build on these, rather than focus – as much of the sector does – on their needs and risks.

We apply the same principle to churches. Sometimes Christians feel inadequate to meet the needs of their community. I remember sitting in Bretton Baptist Church one morning in our early days in Peterborough. There are excellent speakers at Bretton, but during this particular sermon I happened to be looking around and thinking of other things, hopefully inspired by the Holy Spirit. I looked to my left and saw Yvonne and Andy Emery, a couple we were just getting to know. She coached landlords, and he was an electrician-cum-builder – skills perfectly suited to their work of running and owning properties. I looked past them and saw Andy Lanning, the prison chaplain, his jovial demeanour masking his passion for providing for those coming out of jail. I imagined what would happen if the four of us could only sit down together and share our skills and knowledge (our community assets, if you like). Surely, if we shared all those skills, we could make an impact on the lack of housing and care available to ex-offenders upon release. And that is more or less what happened: Yvonne has been a trustee for ten years, and Andy Lanning was a trustee until his death.

My point is this: if those skills existed on one pew, in one church, in one city, just imagine how many unharnessed skills, talents and resources exist in the Church as a whole.

There are many skills that don't seem obviously relevant but are nevertheless ripe for harnessing. We talk a lot about tapping into 'latent financial capital', but finances are certainly not the only resource needed. There may be other things that seem less obvious but are nonetheless key. An example of this was when our IT and website needed to be taken care of and someone in our church was able to provide the skills to meet those needs.

Our available gifts and talents may not be immediately obvious to us. This came home to me on a late summer's day at a Christian festival where I had volunteered to do a talk on mission and outreach for Tearfund (as I still occasionally do). I got up early, drove to the event, and wandered through the mass of tents and poor sanitation that are the telltale signs of a Christian festival – and always remind me of a poorly designed refugee camp. It was raining. Good – more people should come to the talk, I thought. My seminar obviously had an exciting title because at least 12 people turned up. I gave my best impassioned plea for them to believe they could get out there and make a difference in their community.

My message had clearly got through because at the end a woman said to me, 'I don't think our church could do any mission: we're based in a very poor area and a lot of people in our congregation are out of work.'

Quick as a flash, I found myself replying, 'So you're a church rich in time, then.'

My response obviously didn't go down well as she only hardened her position – though I have to admit my point wasn't helped by the smug arrogance and zero empathy with which I delivered it. The conversation continued for a bit, but I realized I had done a better job convincing displaced Muslim Darfurians that they had resources than I had this 'poor' British Christian.

My hope is that those who read this book might be inspired to start or join other initiatives (maybe even Hope into Action?), and that they might be prepared to take some pretty scary toddler-steps and discern God's call. It is tempting, as individuals and as churches, to just stare at the problems of this world and say, 'The issues are too big for our resources. Send them away. Don't clog our church up with them.' Instead, may we rather 'go and see' what we have, and then, with faith and doubt muddled together, bring our limited resources to Jesus and say to him, 'Here is what we have.'[1]

In the feeding of the 5,000, Jesus started – in the same way that much good poverty alleviation does – by asking for an analysis of strengths. Is he also saying to us, the combined Church, 'In the face of so much poverty, with homeless crowds so vast, how many loaves – what resources – do you have?'

47

'Send the crowds away'

As evening approached, the disciples came to him and said,
'This is a remote place, and it's already getting late. Send the
crowds away, so that they can go to the villages and buy themselves some food.'

Jesus replied, 'They do not need to go away. You give them
something to eat.'

–Matthew 14.15–16

It is my conviction that the Church does indeed have something
vital that it can and should be bringing to society. We want to
recognize and release that potential.

I find individual churches inspiring, and the collective Church
even more so. I love the privilege of worshipping in a broad swathe
of churches. I have experienced the Eucharist in High Anglican
churches in ways that have lifted and sustained my spirit for a
full week; I have read a liturgy in a remote windswept church
alongside just six or seven other believers and been moved to
tears by its words. At the same time, I love worship with modern
bands and choruses. I treasure both the tradition and depth of
the former, and the freedom of the latter. As Archbishop Justin
Welby has said, both styles are as good and as bad as each
other. This is very much the ethos we seek to foster at Hope into
Action, bringing together people from across the denominations.
At our conferences, at our services, in our partner churches
and among our staff and volunteer groups, we represent a range
of traditions and believe strongly in God's heart for unity and
oneness.

It is one of my great joys to get together with church leaders. We meet over coffee or simply enjoy a relaxed hour, and I never fail to be inspired by their commitment, humility, sacrifice (48 weekends out of 52 for a start) and desire to build the kingdom of heaven here on earth. Their job description is pretty massive, charging them with responsibilities to prepare services; preach sermons; provide for youth, adults, children and the elderly; support mission, both overseas and at home; fight injustice; evangelize; care for the planet; take baptisms, weddings, funerals. All that, plus dealing with parishioners who have something to say about almost everything.

At times, I sit back and view all that the Church does for society – from food banks to toddler groups, to street pastors, to running schools, to looking after the elderly, to helping countless overseas missions, to supporting over two million people spiritually every Sunday – and think: surely this is the most beautiful, inspiring, eclectic, bizarre, wonderful and exciting sociological feat. Many have predicted the Church's downfall, but Jesus claimed the gates of hell would not prevail against it[1] – a pretty amazing prophecy considering he was also planning to build it on the shoulders of an uneducated fisherman. Throughout the next 2,000 years this collection of volunteers has stuck it out and grown, withstanding the attacks of – to name a few – Pontius Pilate, the Roman Empire, the Renaissance, Stalin, Mao and, more recently, Richard Dawkins. I suspect it will survive our postmodern, post-fact, 'fake news' world as well. If history is a reliable predictor of the future, then investing in the Church is a wise use of resources.

At the same time, churches are also dynamic and fluctuating; they retain their fundamental characteristics while also evolving. The Church is a malleable rock. Thirty years ago few churches had run an Alpha Course, yet now over 20,000 churches in the UK have done so. Likewise, 30 years ago most churches were not using microphones, yet now virtually every church in the land uses them.

Church is dynamic and organic, not static. It is movable by the guiding gusts of the Holy Spirit. We want to be part of a movement that helps lead a new change.

We have seen some of that change, but we want to see it sweep across the Church.

When I think back to my early days, I remember a moment after moving to Peterborough when I was sitting in a church with 200 Christians, not a mile from a hostel for 80 homeless people, and wondering how it was possible that not one person from the church was involved in the hostel and not one person from the hostel was involved in the church. They were two entirely separate and different populations. I began scratching my head. How can this be when there is such a clear and consistent biblical message to serve the poor? I contrasted it with the inspiring church pastors I had seen in Sudan, who lived in the internally displaced people's camps with their flocks.

While these feelings were bubbling inside me, I came upon a book by Bill Hybels called *Holy Discontent*.[2] In it he said that when we are so deeply disturbed by a situation that it won't go away, we should interpret that as a prompting from God that we are meant to be part of the solution. When I realized I felt so disturbed about the separation between the Church and the homeless population, I began to wonder whether this was a God-given 'holy discontent'.

As I pondered it over, I wondered whether part of the reason for these separate populations might be that we have contracted out to charities that which is our responsibility. We've come to the same solution the disciples arrived at: 'They can go to the villages.'[3] We have adopted a paradigm of outreach that doesn't involve us. When a missionary returns from overseas and talks of his or her ministry, most of the time the only responses most people can offer are money and prayer. The same applies when there is an appeal for help with an overseas disaster. This is absolutely the right response (unless God is calling you overseas). However, this approach need not be applied to our own communities: 'You give them something,'[4] comes Jesus' rebuff as he refuses to acquiesce to the easy option.

I have heard people from homeless charities speak at church events and come out with statements like 'Our clients have highly complex needs' or 'They lead extremely chaotic and complicated lives'. I understand, of course, the truth in what they are saying. However, the message they really want you to hear is: 'Our clients are a bit too difficult for you guys to deal with and require our professional input. We are the experts and it's a bit beyond your ability. So let's get down to the unspoken contract here: we would like your money, and that is really the only reason we are here.'

I believe there is a better approach.

Am I not also extremely complicated? I know for certain I am pretty challenging: the reason I know this is that I have a wife who is kind enough to remind me regularly. With this perspective, I avoid calling people 'clients'; I'd rather not see people that way. Can we not give them more dignity, treat them with mutuality, and respect them as equal humans? That is why at Hope into Action we refer to them as 'tenants', as that is what they are. What they need, more than a professional, is relational richness. They need to feel loved, to feel safe, and to feel they have a purpose, a future and a hope. And they need someone to believe in them and to trust them. In other words, they are just like you. For this reason, despite the advice of 'professionals', you *can* actually relate to them and you *can* understand them. A paid professional following an action plan, however good, is not doing that. But a volunteer who is interested enough to be willing to give up his or her free time creates a very different dynamic. When people reach out in love like this, the other person is more likely to feel valued and have self-worth. Churches are full of people with love, wisdom, good social skills, and an ability to understand, empathize and relate. We have so much to offer. It is right that we both offer it and also feel confident that we have something valuable to contribute.

That does not mean that we are muppets in how we approach our tenants – far from it. If the lack of genuine church engagement with those on the edge of society was my first 'holy discontent', then my second was probably this: poorly thought-through outreach.

Both overseas and in the UK, I have encountered too much charity, often from Christians, that is high on passion and low on skill. While the intentions are laudable, the outcomes are at best mixed and at worst harmful, developing dependency while feeding a subconscious superiority in the giver.

I believe God has given us a brain, and that his will, revealed through the Bible, often links knowledge to wisdom and love. Therefore, if we want to show love, we can engage our God-given grey matter to work out practical ways of helping. In this I draw on the letter to the Philippians where the apostle Paul prays for his readers, asking 'that [their] love may abound more and more in *knowledge* and depth of insight'.[5] As the book of Proverbs says: 'I, wisdom, . . . possess knowledge'.[6]

Surely, loving God with all our mind means thinking hard about how we design our outreach.

I am not saying, of course, that this means we get everything right. It doesn't mean we are perfect, and it doesn't mean I haven't made some pretty catastrophic mistakes. But it does mean, at the least, that we try to foster a certain attitude and approach as we seek to extend Christ's love to the world.

If the first area of 'holy discontent' was cocooning ourselves from our duty to the poor by contracting our responsibilities out to other organizations, and the second was poorly thought-through outreach, what was the third? A lack of a genuinely holistic approach.

I was always taught that good poverty alleviation could be judged by whether it is 'giving to' or 'working with'. Overly simplistic, I know, but it is still a good rule of thumb. I remember being told: even in the red-hot heat of a disaster, you should be building your response on the capacities of people in the local community, working with their knowledge and their skills. For example, if we were dealing with a Darfurian child in acute stages of malnutrition, we would still work with the mother to help her cure her child, and we would give her the tools (food, medicine and training) to do just that. 'Giving to' people is fine, and there is nothing wrong in it per se, but it needs to be done as part of a wider approach of releasing them from poverty and empowering them in the process. If we give things to people, we need to be careful we are not robbing them of their dignity, and in turn bolstering our own inner desire to be needed or feel good. I get this wrong the whole time. Therefore, in our training we talk about the internal pull towards being 'a knight in shining armour' or a 'mother hen'; the tendency to assume both of these roles needs to be recognized and resisted.

We had an example of this once when a church offered to give some of our mothers some presents for their children at Christmas. How would you feel, as a mother or father, if someone else chose a gift for your child? I wasn't sure, so I discussed this with a mother in one of our homes – in this case someone who had been used by sex gangs.

She thought about it and turned down the gift, saying, 'I would rather choose my own present. I may not have much, but I've saved up my benefits, and I want the joy of going out there and knowing I have chosen and bought it myself. I'd feel like a bad mother otherwise, and you would be robbing me of the one thing I still have left.'

We therefore turned down the offer from the church. When Christmas arrived, that mother also bought *us* a present, which we gratefully received and in so doing returned her some dignity.

We want to try to love in the way Jesus did. Not a love that is wrapped up in our power of being sorted and not homeless. Jesus didn't love like that. He made himself nothing. He got angry with people who thought they were higher and mightier than others. When a religious ruler thought it was shocking that a prostitute came to see Jesus and even kissed his feet, Jesus praised her and rebuked the man.[7] In effect he was saying, 'What right have you to think of her in such a condescending way?' In the story of Joshua in the Old Testament, the Israelite spies did as Rahab, the prostitute, asked; they respected her.[8] We are worth no more than the lowliest prostitute. Our good works and prayers and tithes do not make us any better than the woman selling herself to fuel an addiction – because we have not earned our salvation; it is given to us by grace. Her sins and rough life do not put her one step behind us in the queue. In fact, Jesus responded to the religious leader's attitude by telling a story about two people who were forgiven debts, and the one who was forgiven more loved more in response[9] – the message being that rather than look down on 'sinners', we, the religious, could actually learn from them. Someone who has been forgiven much loves much and probably has a more intimate relationship with Jesus than I ever will.

In the light of this, we talk of wanting to model mutuality, meaning that we want to approach every relationship as equals. I find that this is a lot harder, and requires more strength, than bossing people about and having the final word. But it is the kind of approach and the kind of love we are after. A humble approach, which, once trust has been earned, allows us to speak the truth to individuals because the recipients know and feel they are not being told off, and that it comes from the mouth of someone who also wants to receive input from them in return.

Thus, our mission is not just to those who are overlooked, but also to the Church. We rejoice in enabling people to get out of their pews and into the lives of the vulnerable. Hopefully, both parties will then meet Jesus. If Jesus lives in us and we model our love on his, then our tenants will meet Jesus in us. Likewise, as we help

227

those in need, we will meet Jesus in them, as he taught us in the parable of the sheep and the goats.[10]

I fear that too often churches have avoided their responsibility to journey alongside people in a relational way by giving to charities or others doing the work. This ducking of the issue is helped by the thinking that one can change a life by giving a one-off gift, when in reality that gift may achieve more in terms of satisfying one's conscience than in really solving a problem. It may also inoculate us against recognizing the need to fully enter the pain of people's lives.

I know some of this may sound like a harsh critique, but it is a true reflection of the thoughts I have wrestled with and which have genuinely troubled me. It is also only paraphrasing a larger discourse out there. Whole books have been written on this stuff.[11] Please don't misunderstand: blessing people with gifts is great – I encourage you to continue doing that – but we should be mindful of the issues around it.

In summary, in setting the foundations for Hope into Action, I felt the following guidelines were important: to empower our tenants (not clients); to have an approach which is thought through, intelligent, relational and empowering; and for people from churches to be confident, take responsibility and engage in relationships. One of the reasons I believe in this is because I believe that by so doing, the churches and church volunteers will grow as well. Christ identified himself with the prisoner, with the stranger, with the hungry and with those on the edge of society, and implored us, in pretty strong terms,[12] to engage with them too. In such a vein, Mother Teresa articulated that she could not have washed the wounds of a peasant for a million rupees; she did it because she realized that she was in fact washing the wounds of Christ. As we meaningfully engage with people who are strange to us – those from a different background or culture – our love expands. Our sense of humanity increases: we become more fully human, more fully who God wants us to be, as we see and love the humanity of another. We've met an angel without knowing it[13] and have flourished as a result.

How is the angel revealed? How do we flourish as humans? I suspect it has something to do with finding our prejudices and fears eroded and replaced by understanding, grace and compassion. We become less closed, more open-minded, less sure of our own 'rightness' and therefore less self-righteous. We lose some of the attributes that maddened Jesus the most. In so doing, we can perhaps begin to make sense of his strange words: 'now that you claim you can see, your guilt remains.'[14]

Few things bring me more joy than meeting someone in prison. I usually enter the gates a little anxious and almost always leave on cloud nine, having had a truly powerful, honest and impactful conversation. I can recall many such encounters now as if they happened yesterday, so seared are they into my memory. I think of the prostitute who told me her life story, so unerringly tragic that it changed me. I remember the drug addict who informed me, 'The thing about druggies, Ed, is that they accept you completely for who you are, without judging you. You can't say that of church people.' Ouch!

I am reminded of the words of a South American prison chaplain whom I heard at a conference: 'I thought God called me into prison ministry to tell people about Jesus. In fact he called me there so I could meet him.'

When God incarnate meets you, you tend not to forget the experience. We meet Jesus in the poor, and when we engage with them we are in fact engaging with the very person we choose to worship. In doing so, we will grow in our knowledge, experience and love of Christ.

In this way, we believe that both our tenants and church volunteers will grow in the knowledge, experience and understanding of Christ when they meaningfully merge. We will meet Jesus who resides in them, and they will meet Jesus who lives in us.[15] There is at best, therefore, an emotional and spiritual transaction. When that happens we have succeeded in our mission, because we define success as church volunteers getting out of their pews, striving to love, and tenants feeling loved.

I remember once sitting outside a cathedral in a city I was visiting and watching as a homeless couple asked to enter. The man on the front door was blocking them from going in, while allowing others to do so. Eventually, someone in a dog collar came and told the pair, in a tone that might have been suitable for something on the bottom of his shoe, to go to the local council to see if they could be housed. I watched as the belittled couple trudged off. I caught up with them, got them some food and then pointed them in the direction of the council.

Homeless people often knock on the doors of churches. Instinctively they turn to the Church, which still represents a space of safety and warmth. Many Christians struggle to know how to respond to them and, as illustrated above, sometimes resort to pointing them to the local council.

We see a time when that is reversed. We see councils beginning to point the homeless to the churches. We see church members all over the UK responding openly, as they have heard Jesus say, 'They do not need to go away',[16] and have seen that providing the poor wanderer with shelter is a part of worship. A home in every community, supported by a church. That is our vision.

Is this the charge Jesus would have us accept? Is he saying to us, 'You've seen the need – now "you give them something"?'[17] Another way of asking that question is: 'Is Jesus calling me to give someone somewhere to live?'

48

'Go and see'

'How many loaves do you have?' he asked. 'Go and see.'

'We have here only five loaves of bread and two fish,' they answered. 'Bring them here to me,' he said.

–Mark 6.38; Matthew 14.17–18

How do we see the Church stepping forward and playing a greater role in society?

We see it happening as the body of Christ takes on board Jesus' teaching about the poor and wealth.

In the aftermath of the 2008–9 financial crisis, there was a lot of talk about how the separation between money and values had contributed to the crash. Jesus told the parable of the talents immediately before talking about the poor in Matthew 25. He linked money, values and the poor, and so should we. But how should we make this connection?

The parable of the rich fool is instructive in this matter.[1] Jesus described the man who stashed away his surplus in barns as a fool. Yet in twenty-first-century Britain, thousands of Christians are doing the same. Billions and billions of pounds of Christian wealth are stashed away in the barns of saving accounts, ISAs, stocks, pensions and second homes across the country. We are fools.

Many of us, myself included, have read that parable many times. We've heard it, but not understood it. Still less, I suspect, acted on it.

Acts 2 and Acts 4 have guided me further: the early disciples modelled a radical way of living where they had 'everything in common' and '*shared* everything they had'.[2] These words terrify us, partly because the richer humans get, the more they feel the need to hoard. It has long been observed that those with virtually nothing share virtually everything, whereas those with a lot share only a little of what they have.

What does this word 'sharing' mean? The root word in Greek is often used to denote community: a community approach to money, or 'community financing' – a phrase a secular donor once used to describe our model. In English we get the words 'sharing' and 'giving' muddled up. If we tell a child to share her sweets, we aren't technically asking her to share them; we are really telling her to give some of them away, while she keeps the rest for herself. She is *giving* her sweets. However, if we tell her to share her doll, all parties involved in the exchange understand that, at some point, she is going to get her doll back. That is *sharing*. In some ways it is more difficult to share than to give because you don't know what the third party is going to do with what you have shared: there is a risk it might come back damaged.

When we put money into banks, pensions (which we all have to do) or stocks, we are sharing it with the rich. The bank takes our money, invests it elsewhere, makes some profit on it and gives us a slice of the returns – and those at the top claim a bonus for doing so. I'm not saying there is anything wrong in that – quite the opposite. Banks are a necessary bedrock of our society, and people charged with the responsibility to manage huge chunks of finance should be rewarded. However, do we need to share *all* our wealth with them? Can we imagine a different economic system in which we don't solely share our capital with the rich? If we want, as surely followers of Jesus do want, to translate the parable of the barns and the example of the apostles into the twenty-first century, how exactly do we do that?

In view of all Christ has given us – the air we breathe, the health in our bodies, the sacrifices he made, the beauty of the environment around us – why not share a percentage, at least, of our wealth with the poor by investing in a home for the homeless? That way we get a sound financial investment while fulfilling the parable of the talents (Matthew 25), avoiding foolishly storing our money in barns (Luke 12), building up our riches in heaven (Matthew 6), providing the poor wanderer with shelter (Isaiah 58), sharing our possessions with others 'as they have need' (Acts 2), welcoming the stranger (Hebrews 13), sharing our second tunic with the person who has none (Luke 3), enriching the Church rather than storing riches where rust and moth destroy (Matthew 6), investing in bricks and mortar, and serving the poor – all in one stroke.

As Søren Kierkegaard said:

> The Bible is very easy to understand. But we Christians are a bunch of scheming swindlers. We pretend to be unable to understand it because we know very well that the minute we understand, we are obliged to act accordingly.[3]

At the time of writing, Hope into Action has over a hundred investors. It is a system that works on many fronts. I and others who have invested capital have a sound financial investment that also serves some of the neediest in our communities, while at the same time building up the Church. Our investment provides both a social and spiritual return, as both tenants and the Church benefit.

How does it work? In short, when someone feels able to purchase a house, he or she retains ownership of the house and then leases it to Hope into Action for five years. We then partner the house with a local church and provide a small monthly cash return over the interim five years. We make a small surplus on each house, which contributes to our running costs.

Of course, most people will not be able to summon up enough cash to buy a whole house themselves. However, that does not mean they can't be involved. In 2012 we had 12 people come together and each invest £10,000 into a house. They each owned one twelfth of the house. Then in 2014 we had over 16 people invest in a home in Suffolk. Some put as much as £25,000 into it and others as 'little' as £2,000, with each owning a percentage share. This was a wonderful example of a church community coming together and, like the early apostles, 'sharing' for the 'needy' in their community.

Most churches probably have, lying dormant among their members, at least enough capital to purchase one house. If a church really is too small, then maybe someone in a nearby church would be able to afford to buy one.

It is our vision that every church in the UK (yes, all 40,000 of them) will purchase a home for the homeless. We foresee, over the next 20 years, a revolution in how Christians use their wealth. At the moment, it is common for Christians to tithe (and we should be proud of that), but what if, as is the case with many Christians, their income exceeds their outgoings? Where do they put their money then? The only real current option open to them is to invest it, effectively sharing it with the rich. Why not share at least some of it with the poor? As government shrinks due to austerity and faces decades of debt repayment, who is to say the Lord will not move so that the churches take the lead and are, once again, at the centre of serving the poorest in our country?

Perhaps then, by sharing our equity, we will build a more equitable society, and we will see 'justice roll on like a river, righteousness like a never-failing stream!'[4]

Will that happen? I have no idea. We would like it to happen, and that is the goal we are working towards. What I know for certain is that the capital is out there, sitting in Christian bank accounts. How do I know that? Not because God has told me in some vision or audible voice, but because I have now spoken to, and received phone calls from, enough people who want to talk because they 'might have a little bit of cash'. After a number of such chats, I know that 'might' means 'absolutely do', and 'a little bit of cash' usually means 'loads of cash'.

Just imagine what our mighty God, more powerful than all the armies and richer than all the governments in the world, would do if we surrendered even a percentage of that wealth to him! It would mean some sacrificial, selfless use of our money – but then isn't that in line with what we pray and sing each Sunday? Are we prepared to put our money where our spiritual mouth is? In view of God's mercy, can this be a way of offering a living sacrifice, holy and pleasing to God, as a true and proper act of worship?[5]

We may not feel we have very much to bring, but perhaps, like the disciples who felt they didn't have sufficient provision, we might hear Jesus ask incisively, 'How many loaves do you have?' And then we may hear him command us, 'Go and see.'[6]

Once we have identified our assets and wealth, we may then hear the gentle invitation of Jesus: 'Bring them here to me . . .'[7]

49

We're nowhere near finished

> Never doubt that a small group of thoughtful, committed citizens can change the world; indeed, it's the only thing that ever has.
>
> –*Margaret Mead*

About two months before we opened our first home, Rach suggested I take a day off for a retreat. I headed out – all the way to my local church – and spent some time in quiet reflection. Towards the end of the day, I began to write down some words that articulated my thoughts, and out flowed the following: 'I have a vision where every church in the land runs a house for the homeless.'

I stopped and looked at the words. They at once terrified and excited me.

I then spent a long time trying to work them out: was this from God, or had it come from somewhere else within me?

As I was thinking about this, I received a letter from Carlos, one of our first two tenants (who was still in prison at the time), in which he quoted from 1 John: 'If we ask anything according to his will, he hears us. And . . . we know that we have what we asked of him.'[1]

The more I dwelt on the idea, the more I thought: how could it not be God's will for his Church to house the homeless? Surely it pleases him if we shelter the afflicted, the imprisoned, the trafficked, the abused, the refugee, and those who suffer the greatest pain, trauma, rejection and isolation – those for whom his heart stirs.

The idea struck me then, and it still strikes me now, as being bang in the middle of God's desires and exactly in accordance with the heart that we see articulated in the Psalms and the prophetic books. Likewise, it strikes me as expressing the heart of this man called Jesus who associated himself with, and healed, those the world overlooked and judged; this Jesus who instructed his early followers not to contract out their responsibilities but to care for the crowds in front of them; this Jesus whose penultimate words were a command to his friend John to take into his home a vulnerable woman. It also seems to me a very good reflection of the way John and the early Christians then lived, as 'they shared everything they had'[2] so that 'there was no needy person among them'.[3] Similarly, I find it an authentic outworking of John's teaching decades later: 'If anyone has material possessions and sees a brother or sister in need but has no pity on them, how can the love of God be in that person?'[4] This is how the early Church operated, and it is how today's Church is still meant to operate.

Thus, I have come to the conclusion that, whatever the source of this idea, it is at least a noble cause, and that there are worse objectives one could put one's energies into.

For this reason, I am glad to now be part of a team that is pursuing this objective. We want to be leaders in a movement where it becomes normal to share one's wealth with the poor by investing in a home. We see a time when it is expected of Christians that, in addition to tithing, they have some investment in a house for the homeless. I am certain the vision is far larger than Hope into Action: we rejoice over any church we hear of that is giving the homeless a home, and wish its members every blessing with it.

Now that we have over 75 homes, people sometimes ask me, 'Ed, did you ever imagine it would get this big?' To which the honest answer is 'Yes!' But that doesn't mean I am not amazed that we have got here. I had a big faith when I started out, and I still do, but I also grossly underestimated how hard it would be. It has been a journey of a hundred thousand tiny steps, countless setbacks, even more disappointments, and relentless wrestles with difficulties.

Having ventured and tussled our way along this road for some time now, we are keen to share the benefits of our journey. We've made tons of mistakes, learned loads and tried to improve our methods along the way. We now have lots of practical tools with which to equip others who are interested – in the shape of policies, procedures, forms and an online manual – as well as having long-term staff members who are imbued with our knowledge and ethos. As we are the only organization that has partnered with over 70 churches to give the homeless a home, we feel we carry a responsibility to wisely share all we've learned. The poor deserve nothing less. We are not yet meeting even a tiny fragment of their needs. It is those unmet needs that must drive us on. With this in mind, we are keen to help any church that is interested in pursuing this idea.

We have improved our vision statement a bit now. It reads: 'Every church lovingly making a home for the homeless'.

If we can love with a love that feels the tragedy of homelessness, with a sense of mutuality in our hearts, and with a desire to share our wealth, our love and our time with the poor, who knows what could happen? If we can collectively follow God's call to provide the poor wanderer with shelter as an act of devotion, heaven only knows the possibilities that lie ahead. If this kind of worship catches on, even half as much as the use of expensive sound equipment (which I am not against), then just imagine what our mighty God can do.

We would have a far richer landscape for the homeless in our country: a society where every church has a home for the vulnerable, supported by a loving, non-judgmental community of local Christians; where the authorities and homeless alike knock at the door of the Church when shelter is needed; where the Church is widely recognized for its leading role in social outreach; where it is as normal for Christians to befriend the lonely as it is to break bread; where providing the poor wanderer with shelter is seen as central to worship.

A society where 'every church in the land runs a house for the homeless'.

It is the least that the poor deserve. It is what God would ask of us.

If you would like to join us in seeing this vision become a reality, we would love to share this exciting journey with you.

What next?

In 2010 Rach and I bought our first house for the homeless and founded the organization Hope into Action, which I now lead full time. The number of homes we run keeps growing, but at the point of writing we have 76 homes in partnership with over 70 churches all over England, from a wide range of denominations.

We try to keep rents affordable so our tenants can find work and still afford to live in our houses. We believe we have one of the lowest rental rates in the nation among homeless charities.

At our heart is a passion to see churches as shining lights across our country, leading the way in responding to the tragedy of homelessness in a real, relational, long-term, sacrificial and highly effective way. We believe churches have enormous power – social power, financial power, spiritual power – to be beacons of hope and action for the homeless in our land, and we believe there is a biblical mandate for them to offer this hope and help.

We want to see a richer landscape for the homeless in this country. We see a time when there is a home in every community, supported by the local church, with each house being a space of dignity, love and supportive, non-judgmental relationships, so that no one goes to sleep at night homeless or unloved.

If you have been inspired by this story in any way, we would love your support.

What next?

We would be very grateful if you were able to support us financially. Please donate as a one-off gift or, even better, every month so your money can help more homeless people receive this wonderful care.

Please also consider praying for us.

If you are connected to a local church, why not consider getting in touch to see if we could partner with you?

Finally, if you have wealth or savings, why not share that wealth with the poor by investing in homes for the homeless?

Further information can be found at <www.hopeintoaction.org. uk>.

All royalties from this book will go to Hope into Action.

If you would like to read more from Ed, you may be interested in his earlier book, *Reflections from the Scorched Earth: A witness from some of the world's toughest war zones*.

Notes

Telling a story

1 See John 8.1–11 (the adulterous woman); Luke 8.43–48 (the bleeding woman).

Introduction

1 Psalm 105.1–2.
2 John 3.21 NIV 1984.
3 Galatians 3.28.
4 In Mark 4.35 Jesus called to his disciples and said, 'Let us go over to the other side.' That is so often the call he gives to us.
5 Matthew 25.31–46.
6 Matthew 25.40.
7 Hebrews 13.2.
8 The feeding of the 5,000 is recorded in all four Gospels: Matthew 14.13–21; Mark 6.31–44; Luke 9.12–17; John 6.1–13.
9 Matthew 6.11.

1 New horizons

1 John Ortberg, *If You Want to Walk on Water, You've Got to Get Out of the Boat* (Grand Rapids, MI: Zondervan, 2001).

2 The man on the bench

1 Isaiah 58.6–7.
2 Isaiah 58.11.
3 Isaiah 58.6–7.

3 An early taste of prison

1 Luke 14.15–24.

2 Luke 14.13–14.

3 In a sermon at the Jubilee+ Conference on 10 November 2018.

5 They were like sheep without a shepherd

1 Isaiah 58.7.

2 Genesis 2.18 NKJV.

3 Luke 4.18–19.

6 A more subtle compassion

1 Luke 4.18.

7 It began with a prayer

1 Colin Salter, *Issues Facing Christians in Sudan Today* (Redruth: Weefour Publications, 2009), p. 250.

2 Luke 1.38 GNT.

3 Psalm 37.4.

8 Doubt steps

1 Theodore Roosevelt, 'Citizenship in a Republic', address at the Sorbonne, Paris, 23 April 1910; cited in Erin McCarthy, 'Roosevelt's "The man in the arena"', 23 April 2015: <https://mentalfloss.com/article/63389/roosevelts-man-arena>.

9 'I have no cows!' – a lie ricocheting down the ages

1 Acts 3—5. The specific quote is from Acts 4.20.

2 Luke 19.40.

3 Luke 4.18–19.

4 See Isaiah 58.6–7 CEV: 'I'll tell you what it really means to worship the LORD. Remove the chains of prisoners who are chained unjustly. Free those who are abused! Share your food with everyone who is

hungry; share your home with the poor and homeless. Give clothes to those in need; don't turn away your relatives.'

5 Amos 5.23–24.

6 Matthew 25.14–30.

7 Proverbs 13.7.

8 See Luke 9.10–17.

10 Stepping stones of encouragement in a sea of fear

1 Genesis 12.1 NLT.

2 Isaiah 30.21.

12 He broke the loaves

1 See Matthew 14.19–21.

14 White-knuckle ride

1 See the story of the parting of the Red Sea in Exodus 14.

16 The father of all rollickings

1 Psalm 32.8 NIV 1984.

2 Luke 9.14.

3 Isaiah 30.21.

18 Mothers

1 In Mark 10.51 Jesus asked blind Bartimaeus, 'What do you want me to do for you?'

19 'For the first time in my life I felt like I was worth something'

1 Different people have advised me to use different terms: one former prostitute has said to me, 'No, Ed, I was a prostitute – use that term'; others have advised the other way round.

20 'We want to show you how much you are worth'

1 Luke 6.36–37.

21 It rips the heart out

1 John 8.11.
2 See John 8.2–11.
3 Psalm 40.2.

22 A mad and dangerous plan

1 A colloquial term used to describe the process of abruptly giving up a drug to which one is addicted, while taking no medications to ease the unpleasant withdrawal symptoms.
2 1 Peter 5.8.

24 'I suggest they pray outside – at 3 a.m.'

1 The Scripture quote is from James 2.14–17.
2 Mark 10.46–52.
3 Mark 5.25–34; Matthew 15.21–28.
4 Isaiah 58.6.

25 'God is there for you in the darkest pit'

1 John 8.1–11.

27 Krish

1 See, for example, Mark 10.45: 'The Son of Man did not come to be served, but to serve, and to give his life as a ransom for many.'
2 Luke 22.50–51; Luke 23.34.
3 In the first recorded speech by anyone after Jesus ascended to heaven, Peter said, 'Repent and be baptised, every one of you, in the name of Jesus Christ for the *forgiveness of your sins*' (Acts 2.38, emphasis added). Peter was later flogged and imprisoned for this and other such messages.

4 The phrases 'quickly fall away', 'wither' and 'choke' come from the parable of the sower in Matthew 13.1–23.

5 Matthew 26.26.

6 Matthew 18.20.

7 Matthew 25.40; see the parable of the sheep and the goats in Matthew 25.31–46.

8 '[We seek] the presence of Jesus . . . in the distressing disguise of the poor.' Mother Teresa, *In the Heart of the World: Thoughts, stories and prayers*, ed. Becky Benenate (Novato, CA: New World Library, 1997), p. 33.

28 'I'll come round and knife you'

1 See Isaiah 40.31.

2 Ministry of Justice, *Costs per Place and Costs per Prisoner by Individual Prison* (27 October 2017): <https://assets.publishing. service.gov.uk/government/uploads/system/uploads/ attachment_data/file/563326/costs-per-place-cost-per-prisoner-2015-16.pdf>.

3 Peter Clarke, HM Inspectorate of Prisons Annual Report 2015–16: <https://justiceinspectorates.gov.uk/hmiprisons/media/press-releases/2016/07/hm-inspectorate-of-prisons-annual-report-201516-prisons-unacceptably-violent-and-dangerous-warns-chief-inspector>.

30 To judge or not to judge

1 See the parable of the prodigal (or lost) son in Luke 15.11–31. The specific quote is at Luke 15.29.

2 Isaiah 58.9.

32 Shame

1 *The Big Issue* is a magazine sold on the streets of cities and towns around the UK, and in other countries, by individuals who are vulnerable and marginalized, often without a permanent home.

The opportunity to earn a legitimate income in this way helps many to regain control over their lives.

2 Merle A. Fossum and Marilyn J. Mason, *Facing Shame: Families in recovery* (New York, NY: Norton, 1989), p. 5.

3 Mark 5.24–34; Luke 23.39–43.

4 Mark 2.1–12.

5 See Mark 5.21–34.

34 Disappointment and joy go hand in hand

1 Jackie Pullinger with Andrew Quicke, *Chasing the Dragon: One woman's struggle against the darkness of Hong Kong's drug dens* (London: Hodder & Stoughton, 2010; originally published 1980), pp. 236–7.

35 Office move

1 The Scripture quote is taken from John 7.38.

36 Our deepest fear

1 John 21.25.

2 See Luke 5.4.

3 Matthew 28.19.

4 Marianne Williamson, 'Our Deepest Fear', *A Return to Love: Reflections on the principles of A Course in Miracles* (New York, NY: HarperOne, 1996), p. 190.

5 John 15.8.

37 'For the first time in years I felt safe'

1 Luke 4.1–13 (emphasis added).

2 Isaiah 58.9.

3 Isaiah 16.3.

4 Exodus 22.21.

5 Hebrews 13.2.

39 'The poverty of being unloved is the greatest poverty'

1 This saying is attributed to Mother Teresa of Calcutta.
2 See the parable of the lost sheep in Luke 15.3–7.
3 Care leavers statistics, in NSPCC Knowledge and Information Service, *Statistics Briefing: Looked after children* (January 2019): <https://learning.nspcc.org.uk/media/1622/statistics-briefing-looked-after-children.pdf>.
4 See Luke 9.3.

40 Rain in the springtime

1 Zechariah 10.1.

41 'Do you know who I am?'

1 Mark 8.36.

43 The cliff face

1 Ephesians 3.20.
2 Mark 4.35.
3 Hebrews 11.1 ESV.
4 Luke 8.22–39.

44 A week in the life

1 Luke 12.13–21.
2 Matthew 25.25.
3 Shane Claiborne, *The Irresistible Revolution: Living as an ordinary radical* (Grand Rapids, MI: Zondervan, 2006), p. 163.
4 Acts 4.32–35.
5 Matthew 7.1.
6 Mark 5.1–20.
7 Matthew 6.33.
8 1 John 4.8.

45 Welcoming community

1 See Luke 10.27.

2 Acts 4.32–35.

3 Luke 6.35–36.

4 Luke 6.37–38.

5 Mark 5.19.

6 Luke 8.39.

7 Genesis 2.18 NKJV.

8 Rowan Williams, *Holy Living: The Christian tradition* (London: Bloomsbury, 2017), p. 19.

9 Psalm 91.9–11.

10 Jackie Pullinger with Andrew Quicke, *Chasing the Dragon: One woman's struggle against the darkness of Hong Kong's drug dens* (London: Hodder & Stoughton, 2010; originally published 1980), p. 236.

11 Luke 19.37–40.

12 Assuming I stayed on my previous salary.

46 Sitting on a gold mine

1 See Mark 6.36–38.

47 'Send the crowds away'

1 'I tell you, you are Peter, and on this rock I will build my church, and the gates of hell shall not prevail against it' (Matthew 16.18 ESV).

2 Bill Hybels, *Holy Discontent: Fueling the fire that ignites personal vision* (Grand Rapids, MI: Zondervan, 2007).

3 Matthew 14.15.

4 Matthew 14.16.

5 Philippians 1.9 (emphasis added).

6 Proverbs 8.12.

7 Luke 7.36–50.

8 See Joshua 2.12–14; 6.22–23.

9 Luke 7.41–47.

10 Matthew 25.31–46.

11 I recommend two favourite books of mine: Steve Corbett and Brian Fikkert, *When Helping Hurts: How to alleviate poverty without hurting the poor . . . and yourself* (Chicago, IL: Moody, 2014); Robert D. Lupton, *Toxic Charity: How churches and charities hurt those they help (and how to reverse it)* (New York, NY: HarperCollins, 2011).

12 See Matthew 25.41.

13 Hebrews 13.2.

14 John 9.41.

15 Colossians 1.27.

16 Matthew 14.16.

17 See Luke 9.13.

48 'Go and see'

1 Luke 12.16–21.

2 Acts 2.44; 4.32.

3 Søren Kierkegaard, *Provocations: Spiritual writings* (New York, NY: Orbis, 2003), p. 35.

4 Amos 5.24.

5 See Romans 12.1.

6 Mark 6.38.

7 Matthew 14.18.

49 We're nowhere near finished

1 1 John 5.14–15.

2 Acts 4.32.

3 Acts 4.34.

4 1 John 3.17.

Scripture acknowledgements

WE HAVE A VISION OF A WORLD IN WHICH EVERYONE IS TRANSFORMED BY CHRISTIAN KNOWLEDGE

As well as being an award-winning publisher, SPCK is the oldest Anglican mission agency in the world.

Our mission is to lead the way in creating books and resources that help everyone to make sense of faith.

Will you partner with us to put good books into the hands of prisoners, great assemblies in front of schoolchildren and reach out to people who have not yet been touched by the Christian faith?

To donate, please visit www.spckpublishing.co.uk/donate or call our friendly fundraising team on 020 7592 3900.

An easy way to get to know the Bible

'For those who've been putting aside two years in later life to read the Bible from cover to cover, the good news is: the most important bits are here.' Jeremy Vine, BBC Radio 2

The Bible is full of dramatic stories that have made it the world's bestselling book. But whoever has time to read it all from cover to cover? Now here's a way of getting to know the Bible without having to read every chapter and verse.

No summary, no paraphrase, no commentary: just the Bible's own story in the Bible's own words.

'What an amazing concept! This compelling, concise, slimmed-down Scripture is a must for anyone who finds those sixty-six books a tad daunting.'
Paul Kerensa, comedian and script writer

'A great introduction to the main stories in the Bible and it helps you to see how they fit together. It would be great to give as a gift.'
Five-star review on Amazon

The One Hour Bible
978 0 281 07964 3 • £4.99